HOW WILL YOU BE REMEMBERED?

A Guide for Creating and Enjoying Your Legacies Now

ROBB LUCY

ALTERNATIVE TITLE:
LEGACIES AREN'T FOR DEAD PEOPLE!

How Will You Be Remembered?
A Guide for Creating and Enjoying Your Legacies Now

Second Edition January, 2017
Original Title – Legacies aren't just for Dead People

Published by Engage Communications Inc.

Ordering information:
Special discounts are available for quantity purchases by corporations, associations, foundations and others.
For details e-mail: stories@createmylegacy.com and you will be contacted within 24 hours.

Interior Design by Krista Gibbard, www.bardillustration.com
Cover Design by Jun Ares
Illustrations by Phil Juliano (www.bestinshowcomic.com) and Roberto Marchionni (www.menotti.com).

Library and Archives Canada Cataloguing in Publication

Lucy, Robb, 1951-
[Legacies aren't just for dead people!]
    How will you be remembered? : a guide for creating and enjoying your legacies now / Robb Lucy. -- Second edition January 2017.

Previously published under title: Legacies aren't just for dead people!
Issued in print and electronic formats.
ISBN 978-0-9940317-2-3 (paperback).--ISBN 978-0-9940317-3-0 (pdf)

    1. Conduct of life. 2. Self-actualization (Psychology). I. Title.
II. Title: Legacies aren't just for dead people!

BJ1589.L83 2016   158.1   C2016-906877-3
                                                C2016-906878-1

Printed in the United States of America

A garden at the end of the street

A well's clean water

Swings in the park

Books in a library

Your story

Grandma's story

A weekly card tournament

Horn lessons in the garage

A life-saving machine in the local hospital

A girl going to school in a faraway country

They're all legacies.

What are mine?
Did I matter?
Was I happy?
Will they remember?

TABLE OF CONTENTS

What They Say VI

What I Say VIII

Introduction

What's it all about, Alfie? 1

W5+H is this book for? 5

1) Legacy Primer

Finding a Definition 11

You talkin' to me? 23

2) Legacy and Life

Time – Hey buddy, spare a minute? 35

Happiness – Your Legacy Smile? 41

Ego – Hey, look what I did! 51

Religion – It Glitters Like Gold! 57

Your Raw Materials – Values, Skills, Talents 65

3) Legacy and Story

So, what's a story? 75

Legacy 1: TELL Your Story 85

Legacy 2: GATHER Their Stories 101
Legacy 3: CREATE New Stories 133

4) Legacy and Sex
The Male and Female Approach 155

5) Legacy and Money
Everyone's a Philanthropist 161
Your New Dance Partners! 169
The Giving Tools 185

6) Legacy 9 to 5
Am I the person my dog thinks I am? 201

7) Getting Started
Your Legacy Journal 209
The First 10 Steps 215
Legacy FAQs 221

8) Your Legacy Smile 2.0 227

Resources and Free Stuff
The Legacy Starter Download 233
Search Terms 234
Acknowledgments 235
About the Author 239

WHAT THEY SAY

"Robb Lucy not only convinces us that we can make our lives better by creating our own legacies, he shows us how to do it. How Will You Be Remembered? is a must-read for anyone seeking to live a more fulfilling life and desiring to leave a lasting legacy."

Boe Workman, CEO Communications,
American Assoc. of Retired Persons (AARP)

"I couldn't believe how it caught my interest. You explained how beneficial our legacies would be to future generations and how to get started. It's easy to read with a humorous touch, great stories and a sense of urgency. A terrific book."

Wilf Wilkinson, Past President, Rotary International

"The book is fantastic for those of us well down our path of life. But Lucy's strategies will be even more influential for my 20-year-old and his generation. Awareness of legacies at their stage in life is powerful."

Ted Singeris, VP Client Relationships, Sun Life Financial

"Robb's book is a generous legacy from a generous man. He gives the reader a tool–a roadmap–to ponder, probe and plan how to use our gifts and skills to have meaningful impact in the world. How wonderful a gift this is!"

Barbara Grantham, President and CEO,
VGH/UBC Hospital Foundation

"Robb is mad for legacies. You could call him a zealot. And he wants you to create one."

Reader's Digest

"Lucy has invented a discipline too often left to guys with tall hats, beards or preachy voices. His book contains many of his notable qualities: explosive brilliance, wit, grace, originality and constant surprises."

Keith Spicer, Journalist & Author, Paris, France

"I was hooked from the opening story. Robb Lucy has a way of grabbing hold of you and not letting go. He writes with great urgency, humor and intimacy. This is a treasure chest of ideas on the most important personal journey you will ever embark upon. You'll be delighted."

Jim Kouzes, co-author, *The Leadership Challenge*

"This book is packed with insight, humor and practical guidance that will help you craft your personal legacy and "story"...and appreciate its value for everyone, now and in the future."

Ross Mayot, VP & GM,
Canadian Assoc. of Retired Persons (CARP)

"A thoughtful and heartfelt exploration of the importance of making your legacy an important consideration in your everyday life."

Robert Galford, Center for Leading Organizations

"A very good, punchy read. I enjoyed doing the self-evaluation (values, skills, talents), and know that creating my legacy now–big or small–is excellent advice."

Mike Harcourt, Premier of British Columbia, 1991–96

"A masterful book...An inspirational and entertaining read... Robb's passion shines through...Three thumbs up!"

Reviews on Amazon.com

WHAT I SAY

Before writing this book, I wondered if anything about my life would be remembered.

I thought I had to be rich to leave a legacy. Um…no, not there yet.

Famous? Nope.

And, I'm not dead yet, which is when most people hear about their mark on life – from their eulogist!

Then life blindsided me. My wife and I lost our only chance of having a family. Both my parents died. And one morning the doctor called and told me I had cancer. I'd never have a chance to leave a legacy. I mean, what could it possibly be?

I started researching, questioning and wondering. What really is a legacy? Does it have to be about money or fame? Will I only know what mine is when everyone at my funeral nods in agreement, "Yup, that's his legacy, alright."

Or, can regular people like me create legacies that positively affect lives, now…and later?

Philosophers and thinkers have taught for eons that all we need to be happy and lead more connected, fulfilled and meaningful lives is to live by our values, using our talents and skills.

Connected? Fulfilled? Meaning? Yikes! Those are big goals. Now, I know your new legacies will help you achieve them.

This book will help you make the best of the rest of your life. If you want to be remembered, this book will act as your legacy guide. After looking at how legacy is reflected in a variety of aspects of our lives (e.g., Who can leave them? Time? Ego? Religion? Sex? Money?), I'll teach you simple formulas for building one, or many, legacies. They might change your life, your neighborhood or the world!

In my seminars people said, "Tell us stories of what others have done." Those stories are here. They'll have you saying, "That gives me an idea!"

I'll demystify and redefine legacy to make it less daunting, more doable and enjoyable. You'll begin to experience the joy of giving, connecting and affecting lives with your legacies.

I wrote this book because people were asking, "What can my legacy be?" I sensed their yearning to find a way to build and enjoy a meaningful life. After you've read this book and you're asked, "How will you be remembered?", I promise you'll have an answer that puts a broad smile on your face because you will know the legacies you've created.

INTRODUCTION
What's it all about, Alfie?

B efore you begin reading, please hum along with Dionne Warwick and me from the 1966 film, *Alfie*.

What's it all about, Alfie
Is it just for the moment we live
What's it all about when you sort it out, Alfie
Are we meant to take more than we give
Or are we meant to be kind, Alfie?

When I heard this song in the '60s it planted a few musical seeds in my brain. *Are we meant to take more than we give? Are we meant to leave something behind?* Something that says, I was here. I'm leaving this for you. And I feel good about it.

These questions, pure and simple, are the questions of legacy. And your legacies, of any size, of any type, are how you'll be remembered. But before delving in too deeply, let me tell you where the examination of legacy really began for me.

After years of trying, and with the help of medical science, my wife, Kim, was finally pregnant. We were ecstatic. I would soon be a father. We walked into the clinic and I held my wife's hand while the nurses prepared the equipment so we could glimpse, onscreen, our six-week-old fetus.

1

"Hey, could you fix it so it's twins, a boy and a girl?" I gushed. "We've got names for them already!"

"Not this time," smiled the nurse, "but maybe next go-round."

The room was alive with energy and anticipation. We were ready for the first view of our little baby. We looked up to the screen.

After a moment, the nurses stopped talking. There was complete silence. The next moment, the energy and joy was sucked out of the room by a big, unseen vacuum.

"What's wrong?" said Kim.

"No heartbeat," a nurse replied.

You ask dumb questions at this point. "What's that mean...?" I said. But we knew.

We cried as we drove home. I held Kim's hand. "We're not going to have a family," she said through her tears.

"Don't worry, we'll get there. I love you. We'll get pregnant," I said. "We *are* having a family."

But over the next couple of years, with all the drugs and science and needles that modern medicine could give us, it wasn't to be. My wife and I wouldn't be parents. I wouldn't be the father I always wanted to be. I wouldn't have a daughter to protect and spoil, or a son to teach how to throw a baseball and fly-fish. And, because I was the only son in my family, our proud Lucy name would disappear. We would have no children to leave our estate to. I wouldn't be able to leave a legacy. It seemed so unfair. My life's legacy had to be about more than having a family.

A few months later, I was walking on the beaches of Normandy with my aging father, retracing his steps from World War II. We visited many of the spots in France, Belgium, Holland and Germany, where very good things and very bad things had happened. It was a trip filled with rich memories for father and son.

The following November, my father was asked to speak about his heroic, story-rich experience of World War II in front of his granddaughter's (my niece's) grade five class. The next time I saw him I asked, "How did it go?"

"Not as well as I would have liked," he said.

Dad wasn't a natural storyteller, and stories were what those 10-year-old kids needed to hear. Over the next year, Dad and I structured 24 stories; every one had the potential to be a movie.

Dad then wrote out each story by hand, including the story of his best friend being killed beside him and the story of receiving the Military Cross from Field Marshal Montgomery. He told the stories of riding into towns in France, Belgium and Holland as victors who freed those cheering people and changed their lives. We reviewed and rewrote the stories. I typed them on my computer, printed them and handed them to my sister, Kathy, a publisher.

We launched my father's book at a military museum. He was a humble and joyful man, and I could feel the immense pride he felt with his story finally in the hands of friends, family and all who wanted a great read.

That book is part of my dad's legacy and is being passed on from generation to generation. I know someone in the future will say, "This is my great, great, great-grandfather's story!"

After this experience, I started to raise the idea of legacy wherever I was. During polite dinners at home, in a restaurant, on a hike and even once while kayaking on the azure Pacific, I asked everyone the same question: "If you 'left' tomorrow, what do you think your legacy would be?"

"I've been too busy to think about it," they'd say. "We've got our kids. I'll get to it later. We don't have the resources or money." Even my fellow kayakers started paddling faster. *Get rid of the legacy guy. He's weird.*

We all know legacy is about leaving "stuff" behind. But what? Everyone I asked was unsure or hesitant, but there was real interest. *Will I be remembered for anything of value? Will my life have meaning? Will others benefit because I was here?*

I could understand the reluctance. Legacy is laden with many weighty ideas: generosity, happiness, relationships, meaning of existence, purpose, love. To combine all that into something we create and enjoy now, which we will leave behind to benefit others. Phew. Tall order.

The lyrics of *Alfie* became a study of legacy, which I found out is a BIG subject. But I learned (again) that, like most things in life, simplicity is the key. I have always told those I worked with, "It's hard to be simple." But, when you get it right, you have greater perspective and enthusiasm to move forward.

I invite you to jump into the future with me. Let's say, a hundred years from now your relatives are talking about you (Great, Great, Great-Grandma Ann, or Great, Great, Great-Uncle Herb). They're talking about a legacy of yours that still resonates in their lives. It doesn't matter what that legacy is (and you'll learn a gazillion options in this book), but they're talking about the *story* of your legacy, a story easily remembered.

With this book, you will be able to create that story, that legacy, once, twice, ten or twenty times.

My first career was as a journalist. Every journalist learns to tell a story with the W5+H. That's: *Who, What, Where, When, Why and How.* I want to start here to show you how this book will work for you.

"Few will have the greatness to bend history itself, but each one of us can work to change a small portion of events, and in the total of all those acts will be written the history of this generation."

– Robert Kennedy

Robb: Or every generation?

WHO is this book for?

It's for anyone who has ever thought, *Hmm...how will I be remembered? Do I want others to benefit from my time here? Do I want to be happier now? Do I want my life to have meaning?*

I'm one of 80 million baby boomers asking these questions. But creating a legacy isn't only for those born between 1946 and 1964. I've met Gen Xs (1965–85) and Gen Ys (1985–2004) who are asking the same questions. The greatest fear for many of us is that we lead a life that turns out to be...well, meaningless, uneventful, uninspiring.

People in my seminars had a hunger. *Tell me what I can do. Inspire me! I want to ensure my life has meaning.*

This book is for people of any age who:
- Wonder what their legacy can be.
- Want to feel connected.
- Want to feel happier.
- Want to be remembered.

WHAT does this book give to people who want to create a legacy?

This book is about being happier *now* as you create your legacies. It's about knowing your life will positively affect those around you, and those you will leave behind.

In my seminars, people told me:
- Keep it simple.
- Make it about life, not death.
- Tell me how. Make it practical.
- Share stories and examples. Excite my imagination to dream something fresh.
- Explain how legacy-building will make me happier.

This book offers an overview. You will learn what skills you have in order to create and enjoy legacy-building. You'll learn how legacy ties into Time, Ego, Happiness, Religion and Sex (all safe if this book falls into the hands of your 14-year-old). I will look at legacy and the financial industry (which would like a piece of what they call "your legacy").

You'll read stories of legacies and then say, "That gives me an idea!" And, one hour after reading this book you'll be able to give your family your first, very powerful, legacy.

WHERE can you build and leave your legacy?

This one's easy. With your family, your community and your country. Thinking of the world? Yes, you can. Legacies can be anything, of any size, of any place. You decide.

WHEN do I start my legacy?

Not to get too panicky about this, but any of us could "go" tomorrow, courtesy of a car accident or faulty heart. You might hear, "Robb was trampled by a rampaging herd of water buffalo." Or, I could "go" in 35 years.

For each of us, the clock is ticking. But, this I *do* believe: It's never too early to build your legacies and start enjoying them. Short answer: Start *now*.

WHY bother with a legacy?

If you were asked, "What will your legacy be?" or "How will you be remembered?", would you have an answer?

Another way to frame the question: Do you want to feel that your life has meaning, and that it will continue to have meaning after you're gone?

Legacies are only talked about when someone dies. Wouldn't it be cool to enjoy building your legacies now, keep them in a journal, and when the time comes for your eulogy, someone proudly reads that journal. "Here are the legacies Robb left behind. And he's proud to tell you what they are."

I think most of us would like to leave a mark on the world. We just haven't given ourselves the time to think about what that mark could be. This isn't about changing your behavior and creating new habits. This book is about you acting out *you*. There are some magnificent things about *you*. You'll learn how to give *you*, then smile broadly.

Socrates said, "The unexamined life is not worth living." Why bother leaving a legacy? Because you have examined your life and you want to say yes to sharing it, yes to being remembered.

HOW will this book help you build your legacy?

This book will act as a guide. It will give you ideas, structure and how-tos, and show you where to go for help. We're changing your question from, "What will I be remembered for?" to "How do I want to be remembered?"

If legacy-building were like crossing a bridge, it would look like this:

You'll first want to understand what a legacy is…and isn't.

You'll then define what your assets are…and how you want to use them to build your legacies.

Then you'll start building your legacies. You'll learn how to TELL, GATHER and CREATE them…and the stories that naturally come with them.

And then you'll reach the other side and realize the huge benefits of legacy creation: being more connected and happy, feeling your life has meaning and renewed purpose.

Phew! A big promise, yes? And here's another one: You might get to know yourself better. As Carl Jung said: "He who looks outside, dreams. He who looks inside, awakens."

There's work to do as you read this book, but when you're finished you'll really pick up speed with the FREE download of *The Legacy Starter* at www.createmylegacy.com.

Or, you can wait for your eulogist to try and figure out what your legacies are. *Um, so far as we know, he was working on the stampede habits of water buffalo.*

So, that's Who, What, Where, When, Why and How it's all about, Alfie.

Now, what is a legacy? How would you define it? Let's explore that.

LEGACY PRIMER
Finding a Definition

*"What lies behind us and what lies before us are
small matters compared to what lies within us."*

– Ralph Waldo Emerson, American essayist, poet and thinker

I think legacy may be the most overused, least understood word in the English language. What does legacy really mean? For the first model, I head to the dictionary.

Dictionary Model

1. A gift by will, especially of money or personal property
   Synonyms: bequest, devise, inheritance
2. Something handed down by an ancestor or predecessor.
   Synonyms: birthright, inheritance, patrimony

So, legacy is about money and death? Someone's got to die to create a legacy? How uplifting. Die, leave your money and bingo! Legacy! Sadly, this is the most common perception. Plus, on your way to building that legacy there are estate planning and planned-giving specialists who will help you package up your legacy (for a fee), to ensure a nice gift lands on the laps of your beneficiaries after you say your final "good night."

I think there are a few other legacy models we should explore before creating our own definition.

Philanthropist Model

In the daily media you often read of philanthropists who have made major contributions to their community or country. God love 'em. But, to leave a legacy, do you have to be rich or famous, or both? Without the high profile or big income, a person might think they can't make the world a better place. So, no legacy?

Hero Model

Legacies are often viewed in the context of great heroes, legends or icons. Think Napoleon, Beethoven and Lincoln, their contributions preserved in our history books. The legacy of Martin Luther King, Jr.? Easy, the emancipation of African Americans. Dr. Frederick Banting? Insulin. The Wright Brothers? Flight. Nelson Mandela? A changed South Africa. You might even consider that little Apple computer to be the legacy of Steve Jobs.

But, all these legacies seem rather...um, big. I think most of us need a definition of legacy that will allow us to start at a more manageable level. But first, let's push on through the other models.

Media Story Model

The media (especially sports) tells us about new "legacies" daily. Like the legacy of the quarterback who threw the most winning passes. Are those passes a legacy? Do sports records change lives? They're a memory, a record, but a legacy? Then there are the stories of the cultural, business, environmental and scientific achievements announced every day. Some are immediately called legacies. Legacies? I'm not sure.

Family Model

You might think, *It's all well and good, but my kids are my legacy.* You instilled values, you nurtured, you taught and you loved. I wish I'd had that chance. Yes, your kids are your legacy if that notion fits your definition. But you're not done yet. So, consider this: you can be very proud of your kids, but you can't take direct credit for what they do. Let them go out and create their own mark in the world, their own legacies. Now's the time to create more of your own.

Do a search for legacy on the Internet and you'll come up with hundreds of millions of results, most of them cozying up to legacy's powerful concept, perhaps to be seen as kinder, wiser and more important than each of them really is.

I saw a truck with the proud identifier running the length of the box: *Legacy Grease Trap Maintenance.* How low can a great idea go? Clearly, we need a definition.

David King, chair of The Giving Institute, agrees that most people think creating a legacy is daunting. "They can be overwhelmed, thinking that legacy needs to be large. We need to redefine it so legacy is much simpler; so it's something we create that lasts."

How I found legacy

I hadn't thought too much about legacy until I flew across the country while sitting beside a colleague I didn't know very well at the time. I told him I was going to receive a national award for the charity work I'd done.

We also talked about my dad's book and he said, "That's quite a legacy you've got." I thought he was crazy. We talked for five hours about what legacy could be. We were still talking about it when we caught separate cabs.

Legacy was in my brain to stay.

Remember *Star Trek,* and the credo they all lived by, the Prime Directive? Kirk, Spock and all who followed agreed there could be no interference with the internal development of alien civilizations.

The Prime Directive in the animal world is to ensure and preserve the next generation. My wife and I have started raising honey bees. Nobody works harder than our little bees to create the honey to feed themselves during the winter, and start again in the spring. And, if the queen doesn't make it, the remaining bees make another queen. The Prime Directive is to keep on keepin' on.

Sigmund Freud said that the primary human motivation is the avoidance of pain. You may be right Sig, but there's another way to look at it. Dr. John Izzo, author of *The Five Secrets You Must Discover Before You Die*, believes that the primary human drive is the search for significance; the desire to know that your life and work matters. Izzo says our Prime Directive (when we're in touch with it) is to make our life, and our descendants' lives, better. We're part of this beautiful experiment called life, and our Prime Directive is to extend it, to make it better than when we found it.

The different kinds of legacies you'll learn about in this book will confirm how you lived and made a difference. Each of your legacies will be a gift to yourself today (making you happier), and a gift for the future (part of our Prime Directive). And legacies last. Just knowing that brings joy and energy to the act of creating them. We're more aware of our carbon footprint, but shouldn't we pay just a little more attention to our legacy footprint?

How about that definition?

Let's create our own definition of legacy to give us some direction. Later, you will consider, *Is this a legacy? Does this fit with what I believe a legacy is?* You don't have to agree with this definition. You can change it. Here are a few ideas from great minds to get us started:

IDEA
#1
Connection

"It is one of the most beautiful compensations of this life that no man can sincerely try to help another without helping himself."

– Ralph Waldo Emerson

So, should I enjoy my legacies too? You may have heard the phrase, "The one who plants the tree rarely enjoys its shade." But I do want to enjoy the shade with others. That's the joy of life, isn't it? Laughing, bonding, doing, connecting…together.

IDEA
#2
Pay it Forward

"The great use of life is to spend it for something that will outlast it."

– William James

Ah, create and leave it for others to enjoy. Like Dr. Amit Goswami says in *Physics of the Soul*, "The purpose of life is to learn, to love and to be creative, to develop that which survives physical death."

IDEA

#3

Stories

"As long as our stories live, we live."

– Irish proverb

My great-grandparents were Irish immigrants who came over to Canada around 1875 and scratched a living out of the poor soil in Northern Ontario, while some of their kin headed to Philadelphia. I'm sure they believed in this bit of Irish lore: lasting legacies produce stories that last too. I believe it. I guess that's the South Cork blood flowing in me.

So, by combining ideas: 1. Connection, 2. Pay it Forward, and 3. Stories, here's the definition of legacy we're building on.

A legacy is something I create that connects and enhances lives now, and will continue to positively affect others when I'm gone.

So, with this definition in mind, I looked around my world to see if I could spot some legacies, and this is what I found:

- Injured in a car accident and confined to a wheelchair, an athlete is focused on finding a cure for spinal cord injuries.
- A fireman is taking kids out of violent lives with rock and roll.
- A tax-smart individual supplies resources to ensure a charity has the structure and skills to meet its goals.
- Grandpa teaches tweens about decision-making with eggs and a checkerboard.
- A lady learned to enjoy her legacy in the park now, instead of leaving it in her will.
- A young lady is changing the lives of girls in Ghana, and loving it.
- A Legacy Letter brings a family together, finally.
- Annual flowers along a country road put smiles on people's faces each year, and will long after the gardener is "planted."

. . . .

Hmm. Maybe I don't need to be rich, or have kids or have changed the lives of thousands to leave a legacy? Studies show that when you tap into your values, skills and talents, you'll experience a deeper happiness, a happiness you might never have known. I'll sprinkle legacy stories throughout this book, confirming that a little idea can have a big effect. These will be *Hey that gives me an idea!* examples of legacies.

And you don't have to do it by yourself. I'll tell you a story later, of how neighbors came out of their houses to make my small legacy theirs too. It connected us. Plus, if your legacy idea fits with them, charities and foundations are there to help you, and will be delighted to ensure your legacy becomes real.

Let's go to the future, to your eulogy. Wouldn't it be kind of sad if the eulogist has to dream up your legacies? Instead, why not leave a nice, tidy list of legacies that made you happy, connected you to others and made other lives better? Now, that's how to be remembered!

We all live unique lives, with the ability to leave a full and defined footprint. I want to help ensure your legacy story will be part of a conversation 100 years from now, even though you won't be there.

John Kotre, author of *Make It Count: How to Generate a Legacy that Gives Meaning to Your Life*, told me that he believes there's nothing too small, it's never too soon and it's never too late.

Kotre calls legacy-building "Generativity" – a feeling of mattering, of creating lasting value, of passing yourself to others. Generativity revolves around the fact that we are reproductive beings who wish to be fertile, urged by our very genes to multiply and populate the earth. As humans, we do that in more than a physical sense. Kotre says we do it with our craft and our care, with our hands and our genius. We do it as parents, teachers, shepherds, guardians and guides; as artists and scientists and enactors of ritual; as responsible citizens and movers in our businesses and communities. We do it when we bear fruit, sow seeds, create legacies and leave the world a little better off for our presence in it.

Is there such a thing as a negative legacy? Unfortunately yes. Think of Pol Pot in Cambodia, or Hitler in Europe, or the legacy of the very mixed-up kid with a gun in a school or theater. But, enough of the negative.

While sitting in your rocking chair years from now, you may ask yourself, *What is my legacy?* Which of your values, skills and talents will you use to build legacies that *you* will enjoy? Legacies that will connect you to others who will continue to enjoy them after you say your final "good night"?

Can you name the last three Grammy Award winners for Song of the Year? No? Okay, how about the names of the starting quarterbacks in the '67, '75 and '98 Super Bowls? If you're like me, you might have a problem with these. But, if I asked for the name of the teacher, neighbor or friend who positively impacted your life, I'd guess you'd have very little trouble coming up with names. The lesson? Fame doesn't make a legacy, effect does.

Unfortunately, I've buried a few friends, some of them dying at the peak of their game. They were healthy, and had plans. There's a Sanskrit quote that goes something like this:

"Spring has passed, summer has gone and winter is here. But the song I meant to sing remains unsung. I have spent my days stringing my instrument."

Your songs, your legacies, are ready to be sung. You have the values, talent, skills and resources to make yourself happier and make a difference in other's lives. And the time to start is, you guessed it, *now*. You don't have to die to leave a legacy. The desire to create and leave a legacy, a gift from you to the future, is as timeless as humankind. If you believe you're part of something bigger, wouldn't it be pretty cool to add to that bigness with even the smallest of legacies? Something to live on after you've gone? Something to add to our Prime Directive? Because you're reading this book, I'll bet you answered, "Yes, yes, and yes!"

So, this sums up the definition of legacy that we've been building on:

Your legacies will *connect* you to people, will enhance your life and theirs... and will continue to positively affect lives when you're gone.

The switch in our thinking is that we get to enjoy them *now*, knowing we'll pass on some good things even after we "go."

Now, who's more predisposed to leave a legacy? You? Your parents? Your kids? Who are we to be thinking about legacy?

You Talkin' to Me?

You talkin' to me?

Okay, now we have a definition of legacy. So, who's creating these legacies? Who *can* create them? For perspective, let's look at four groups as recognized by demographers at the Joint Center for Housing Studies at Harvard University. Then we'll look at the group that I, and probably you, belong to.

Silent Generation (Traditionalists), born 1925-1945

They knew the Great Depression, segregation, World War II and the G.I. Bill. Their values and traits are patriotism, loyalty, selflessness and waste not, want not.

Baby Boomers, born 1946-1964

They knew the postwar economy, civil rights, Vietnam War, Cold War, the antiwar movement and the beginning of the Computer Age. They hold values and traits of optimism and idealism, equal rights and activism. In 2030 every Boomer will be over 65, about 20% of North America's population.

Generation X, born 1965-1985

They knew Watergate, Iran-Contra, AIDS, the Space Shuttle Challenger explosion and started careers near the beginning of the Computer Age. They are independent, resourceful and skeptical about government.

Generation Y (Millennials), born 1985-2004

They knew Oklahoma City, Columbine, 9/11, the Internet, Katrina and social networking. Their values and traits are realism, pragmatism and diversity. There were 17 million more Generation Ys born than Boomers, and there are 27 million more Generation Ys than Generation Xs.

Some Boomer Facts

If you're thinking about legacy now, chances are you're a Boomer. I am too – one of about 84 million born in the U.S. and Canada during the "boom years," 1946–1964. Actually, Canada's baby boom ended in 1966 as Canadian servicemen came back from Europe a little later than U.S. soldiers. During the baby boom in North America, a baby was born every seven seconds. That was about 12,300 babies per day, or 4.5 million babies per year.

We were the kids born into a robust postwar economy. We learned about the world on those brand new black and white television screens. We became optimists and idealists, on the streets for civil rights, the women's movement and the sometimes violent antiwar protests. We know where we were when those shots rang out in Dallas and when Armstrong walked on the moon. We watched Khrushchev pound his shoe and we prepared for mushroom clouds in our cities as the Cold War got hot.

Boomers account for 50% of consumer spending. We buy 80% of health care products and we comprise 60% of voters. A 60-year-old has a 50% shot at reaching 90. We've gathered tremendous amounts of material wealth, courtesy of our own efforts and our parents' estates (more on that later).

Because our life expectancy is greater now, never before in Western society will so many people reach their seventh decade. Life expectancy will be about 87 years for men, and 90 years for women. In 1900, it was 47 years for each.

And now you've got this book in your hands because you know it's time to figure out what your legacies can be. The early Silent Generationers may have wrapped up their legacy-building, but everyone forward of that, Boomers, Generation Xs and Generation Ys and beyond, hang tough. At some point each group will want to know how to leave the mark of a meaningful life.

John Izzo (*The Five Secrets You Must Discover Before You Die*) calls us the "Lucky Suckers," saying it's time for us to step up and take on some big problems, like our environment and overpopulation. By 2034, the last of the Boomers will be out of the workforce. As we reach the final lap in the race, what will we have to show for it? What story will each of us have to tell?

The Challenge for Boomers

While sitting in my rocking chair, I might ask myself, "How did I affect the world? Will my deeds continue to enhance lives when I'm gone? Did my life have a purpose?"

"Boomers are in the legacy-crafting business," Bill Novelli told me. The former CEO of the American Association of Retired Persons (AARP) also said, "It is *the* biggest opportunity of our lives."

Novelli is co-author with Boe Workman of *50+: Igniting a Revolution to Reinvent America*. They say that, yes, we're going to live longer than our parents, and we should seize the opportunities that spring from our increased longevity. We can transform and improve not only our own lives, but also society, dramatically, and for the better.

"My thesis is, legacy is powerful," Novelli told me. The challenge for the largest retirement-age generation in history is to grasp the unique opportunity that faces us. Novelli and Workman argue that we are at a unique moment in time when the need for change coincides with the Boomers' ability to create change. The biggest demographic bubble in history has the time and resources to stir things up.

"People want to give back," Novelli said, "they just have to know they can, and then learn how. We have to ask ourselves, 'How do I want to be remembered?'"

Yes, middle age will have its effect, physically, financially and socially. We'll be going over different speed bumps in our 50s, 60s and 70s.

"We should be excited," said Novelli. "It's a quest. Our lasting legacy should be to leave the world a better place, to finally give back more than we've taken."

The Legacy Focus for Boomers

In the early part of this century, the financial legacy-building by most Boomers was thought to be quite realistic; we were going to be beneficiaries of the biggest wealth transfer in history. Though the recession beginning in 2008 undoubtedly shaved it, this intergenerational transfer of wealth to the Boomers from their parents was estimated to be between $30 to $135 trillion. The Center for Retirement Research at Boston College says it will run around $40 trillion by 2052.

A study published in early 2011 for MetLife estimated that two-thirds of Boomer households will receive some inheritance, with a median of $64,000. High-wealth households can expect to receive an average of $1.5 million, compared to $27,000 for those at the lower end.

And, most interesting, it seems the amount received by Boomers, adjusted for inflation, could be about the same as that received by adult children of the same age back in 1927–1945. Who'da thought?

Strangely, Boomers aren't consumed with the pot at the end of their parents' rainbow. In 2005, *The Allianz American Legacies Study* revealed that 2,600 Boomers and their elders were asked how they define leaving a legacy.

"This national survey found that for the overwhelming majority, legacy has to do with deeper, more emotional issues," said Ken Dychtwald, a research consultant at Age Wave who managed the study. "An inheritance focuses primarily on the money, but a true legacy also includes memories, lessons and values you teach to others over a lifetime."

The most important part of legacy was the sharing of values and life lessons, according to 77% of Boomers and 77% of their elders. In a 2012 reprise study, even after the financial crisis that began in 2008, people felt the same: 86% of Boomers and 74% of elders still felt the sharing of values and lessons through "family stories" was the most important part of legacy. Financial inheritance was quite low – 9% for Boomers and 14% for elders.

Oh, the changes!

If you're a Boomer like me, you might have noticed a few changes coming down the pike in your own life. Geriatric psychology expert David Solie says that Boomers should be ready for a psychological riptide. "Complex and confusing currents will undo many successes of the first half of life" he says. Yikes!

First, will be what he calls the "external forces." Death of our parents, and with increasing frequency, other family and friends. Then, loss of our health, jobs and career. You get the idea.

I do. Both my parents are now gone. I've fought cancer. I sometimes wonder where the career should go.

Some of my friends are really getting the squeeze, with one or both parents in retirement homes, which are not inexpensive. They try to find time to visit while at the same time hold down jobs, and often spot the odd bit of cash to their 30-year-old kids who have moved back home when out of work. This puts a lot of stress on the late Boomer. Solie says one of the primary tasks for Boomers in middle age is to, "Maintain stability in a world of increasing personal volatility."

Then there are the "internal forces", which include questions of purpose and direction for the second half of life. When we entered the first half of life's stadium, society was there cheering us on to great accomplishments. In the second half of life, Solie says that Boomers may be surprised at how small the crowd has become, and how it can be surprisingly silent. "The Boomer's second task in middle age," says Solie, "is to discover purpose and direction."

I think part of that joyful, fun, energetic direction is legacy-building. *If* a small percentage of the 80 million or so Boomers in North America work to leave legacies that positively impact others, well, the world could be a different place. Legacies don't have to be hospital wings or worldwide charities. Smaller legacies can also have a big effect.

Remember our definition of legacy is to create something, "that connects and enhances lives" and also to *create it now* so you and those around you can enjoy it. Don't wait till you're lying in palliative care wondering what the heck the eulogist is going to say about you.

Human Potential Phases

Dr. Gene D. Cohen was a pioneering psychiatrist who researched geriatric mental health at George Washington University. He died in 2009, but left us with his book, *The Creative Age: Awakening Human Potential in the Second Half of Life.* Cohen believed that his "human potential phases," each one shaped by our chronological age, history and circumstances, promote new possibilities later in life. Each phase can help close the gap between recognizing your potential and harnessing it. But, this doesn't mean *lie back and watch it happen.* These phases don't automatically produce growth or creativity. Your legacies' potential will be realized through your own efforts or through the help of others.

Mid-life Re-evaluation Phase

This phase generally occurs when you're in your early 40s to 60s. Today, this phase is filled with Boomers and Generation Xs. In less than 10 years, Generation Ys will be in this phase. Mid-life combines insightful reflection and a powerful desire to create meaning in life. We confront mortality for the first time. We begin to re-evaluate our sense of purpose, plans, actions, relationships and our path in life, enabling us to uncover our unrealized creative side. We consider questions like: *Who am I? Where am I going?* And a different question: *Where have I been?* We're less impulsive, more open to new ideas and have greater respect for our intuition.

Liberation Phase

This phase emerges when you're in your mid-50s to mid-70s (in 2016, the Boomers and some of the Silent Generation). We've got a new sense of personal freedom, feel free to speak our minds. There are liberating feelings and thoughts of, *If not now, when? Why not?* and *What can they do to me?* There's a sense of finally having time to experiment with something different, to take a risk, to innovate, to express yourself. This new sense of confidence and courage translates into creative expression for many, sometimes for the first time.

Summing-Up Phase

This phase unfolds mostly at age 70 or older (in 2016, the Silent Generation). We feel a more urgent desire to find larger meaning in the story of our lives through the process of looking back, summing-up and giving back. As "Keepers of the Culture" we want to contribute whatever wisdom and wealth we may have accrued to others. Our creative expression often includes writing an autobiography, personal storytelling, philanthropy, community activism, volunteerism and other activities of giving back. The summing-up process also leads to an account of unfulfilled dreams and unfinished business, and that can lead to a new creative burst to complete the missing chapters in our life story.

Encore Phase

This phase occurs in our 80s and older (in 2016, the Silent Generation). In this phase, there's a desire to make a lasting contribution, affirm life, take care of anything unfinished and celebrate personal contributions. You may encounter powerful desires for love, companionship, control, self-determination and giving back. There is a vitality of the spirit and excitement about life despite the obstacles. You affirm life and celebrate your place in family, community and in the spiritual realm.

As a Boomer, I'm in the Liberation Phase, thinking creatively and asking, "If not now, when?" If that's you too, you're on the launch pad for a legacy flight. Your imagination and your brain will benefit from the activity that legacy-building involves. It's called "brain plasticity." Yes, our brains will grow with new external and internal stimulation. Old dogs can, and *do*, learn new tricks after all.

One weekend, some of my family were at my sister's beautiful place alongside the Kootenay River in British Columbia. I asked my then 94-year-old father what he thought his legacies were. I thought I knew what they were, but wanted him to tell me. As a humble man, he struggled and said he'd think about it. We never talked about it again. He died eight months later.

I want to know what my legacies are. I can feel a bit of that riptide Solie talks about: loss of health, death of parents and friends, change of career, etc., so I'm focussing on them and those big ol' concepts of purpose and meaning. Whether Silent Generation, Boomer, Generation X or Generation Y, each of us will come to a point in our lives when we wonder whether we should *save* or *savor* the world. I'm ready to try a little of both.

Now, remember when I said that one of the excuses I most often heard was, "I haven't had time to think of legacy?" The obvious question then is, "When will you find that space in your life?" Is there any hurry? I mean, I'm fairly young. I've got lots of time. *Don't I?*

LEGACY AND LIFE
Time – Hey buddy, spare a minute?

"I'm older now
I have more than what I wanted
But I wish that I had started long before I did."

– Crosby, Stills and Nash, *Wasted on the Way*

My brush with ill health made me a lot more aware of the clock. Let's call it the Legacy Clock.

Playwright George Bernard Shaw said that the ultimate statistic was, "One out of one dies." If we accept that as a fact, there are two implications: First, because we will die, we need to pay attention to how we live. Second, if we care about anyone, we need to think about leaving something of ourselves behind that just may make their life better.

But does each of us have the time to build our legacies? I guess if I want the happiness that legacy-making can bring, it's time to get to work! I'll do my legacy timeline first, then it's your turn.

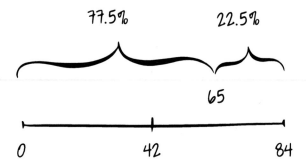

On the line above, I've written 0 on the left to indicate my birth. On the right, I wrote the age I think I'll get to – 84. I think I can get at least another 19 years out of the ole chassis. I'm swimming, biking, golfing, kayaking and eating well to up the odds. Then I noted my life's halfway point – 42. My current age is 65.

Now the percentages.
I'm 65/84ths, or 77.5% through my life. I've got 22.5% to go, 19 years, if all goes well.

Yikes! And those 19 years are not guaranteed. It could be one or two. I could be beamed aboard an alien ship tomorrow, hunted down by a grizzly bear, struck by a meteor or just hampered by poor health, which will be a common problem for many of us. Never mind the water buffalo! If there's even one little legacy I can create that brings joy, and that benefits me and those I leave behind, well, I'd better get going on it.

"Many people die with their music still in them. Why is this so? Too often it's because they're always getting ready to live. Before they know it, time runs out."

– Oliver Wendell Holmes, Sr., American physician and poet

Okay, your turn. Use a pencil on this page.

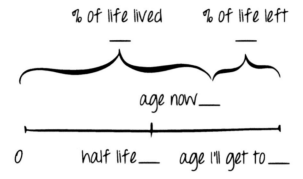

- On the right put down the age you think you'll get to.
- Enter the age you'll be when halfway through your life.
- Enter the age where you are now.
- What percentage of your life have you lived so far? (Age now divided by age I'll get to).
- What percentage of your life have you got left? (100% minus % of life lived).

After reading a few more chapters you'll have a variety of legacy ideas. And now you know the number of years you've got to complete them if all goes well!

> *"There is a brisk energizing of the soul when you really face up to your own existence."*
>
> – George Santayana, American philosopher

One of the three kinds of legacies you'll learn about is collecting the stories you don't want to disappear. For now, pick one person in your life whose story you'd like to ensure is not lost.

Pick a parent, grandparent or that wild and crazy uncle who led quite a life. Their story will be enjoyed by you, your family and friends, and future generations. That story could be a one-pager, a book or a feature-length film. You'll learn more about these options later. For now, just pick one person you who know has a great story, a story you don't want to disappear.

My Storyteller: _____

Next time you see this person, show them your graph and ask them if they would fill in their numbers with you. What percentage do they think they have left? If all goes well you'll have some time to collect their story, although this isn't always the case. After completing my dad's book, I wanted to collect the stories of two more people. One of them passed away two months later. I'm still working on the other one, and won't let the Legacy Clock ring its alarm of "too late."

This poem was found in the pocket of Al Capone's lawyer, Easy Eddie O'Hare. Easy Eddie was taken down by a blaze of gunfire on a lonely Chicago street because he had ratted on Capone. He was trying to make good so his family would be proud of him. Tragic, yes, but his story lives on.

The clock of life is wound but once
And no man has the power to tell
Just when the hands will stop
At late or early hour.
Now is the only time you own
Live, love, toil with a will
Place no faith in time
For the clock may soon be still.

So, we've discovered that time can be our friend...and sometimes a bit of a pest. It's a reminder that legacy-building shouldn't wait, except for when you're driving your car (with apologies to Ogden Nash):

Beneath this slab
John Brown is stowed
He watched his phone
And not the road.

Before you even wonder if you've got the time, you might think, *Why bother?* What's the point of dreaming up and creating your legacies, whether tiny or humongous? These legacies won't do much for you, right?

"Ah, non Alphonse," I say in my best French. In the next chapter, you'll find that these legacies will also create a très, très happy you.

Happiness – Your Legacy Smile?

I had the opportunity at a conference to ask the Dalai Lama that simple question: "Why are we here?"

"To be happy!" he said, followed by that boyish laugh. "But remember," he cautioned me while he played with the small yellow scarf tied to his deep red tunic, "Happiness is not something ready-made. It comes from your own actions."

I knew he'd said this many times, to many people. I was left with three $64 zillion questions:

1. What is happiness?
2. How do I get happy?
3. What is the connection between legacy and happiness?

1. What is Happiness?

> *"The pursuit of happiness holds an honored position in American society, beginning with the Declaration of Independence, where it is promised as a cherished right for all citizens."*
>
> – Sonja Lyubomirsky, author of *The How of Happiness*

Being happy is one big business. The week I wrote this section there were over 64,000 books on Amazon that dealt with some aspect of personal happiness, including *The Art of Happiness* by the aforementioned Buddhist monk. And if you're looking for a speaker to make you smile, try one of the hundreds of thousands of Google listings found under "motivational speakers, happiness." There are books, blogs, quizzes, online courses, weekend retreats and Lord knows how many billions of hours spent on psychiatrist, psychologist and psychoanalyst couches. We want to know how to find happiness, quantify it, and repeat whatever's necessary to get there again! The advice rings all around us. You'll be happier if you: Count your blessings. Be with friends. Savor life's joys. Clean your closet. Sleep more. Etc. Etc. Etc.

Geez, couldn't it just be as simple as, "Don't worry, be happy," as Bobby McFerrin sang? Maybe happiness would fall upon us if we'd just stop fretting?

Depending on the psychologist you talk to, happiness is:

- The degree to which you judge the overall quality of your life.
- A feeling of being in control, while affirming; *I want this to continue.*
- A combination of pleasure and meaning.
- A sense of personal growth.
- A feeling of connecting or contributing to others.

Our old friend Aristotle agreed that, "Happiness is the meaning and the purpose of life." He studied *eudaimonia*, which is Greek for happiness or human flourishing. So, if you want to be happy, call yourself an eudaimoniac.

The experts (psychologists, psychiatrists, neuroscientists and Buddhist monks), agree *real* happiness has depth to it. That means living a meaningful life, using your skills and other assets to connect with people and live a life of purpose.

But, weren't you born happy? Didn't your parents have anything to do with your innate level of happiness? Well, researchers have found that we inherit around 48% of our natural happiness from Ma and Pa. So when you get grumpy, you can blame them.

2. How do I get happy?

My friend Ken and his wife Cathy walked up to their car, only to find a meter maid writing a ticket. Ken was angry.

> *"Most folks are usually about as happy as they make up their minds to be."*
>
> – Abraham Lincoln

Cathy said, "Chill dude." She grabbed some dimes and quarters from the change pocket in the car. As the meter maid was writing their ticket she walked up the street ahead of the meter maid plugging every meter that was out of time.

She came back to the car beaming. "That was worth it," she said.

Cathy died a few years ago, but Ken always plugs a few meters with a smile on his face to remember her.

The happy business seems to focus on *happiness boosters*. Boosters are kind of the "pay it forward" concept, like filling the empty parking meters, or depositing the road toll for the guy in the car behind you. I'm happily married, but I'll still tell a woman in a bank lineup or a cashier in a store that, "You look great in that color. Are you a Spring?" It shocks the heck out of them, but I learned about colors while producing materials for *Color Me Beautiful* early in my career.

One experiment I ran across measured people's happiness levels and then challenged them to talk to strangers in elevators for a week. By week's end, their happiness score was up substantially. An act of kindness is another happiness booster, like mowing a neighbor's lawn, or shovelling their walk. You'll feel great, and it'll be good for you too.

"The most effective way to turbocharge your joy is to make a 'gratitude visit,'" says Dr. Martin Seligman, the Director of the *Positive Psychology Center* at the University of Pennsylvania (www.authentichappiness.com). "This could be writing a note to a teacher, parent, pastor, grandparent or friend, letting them know the value they've added to your life. Deliver it, or visit and read it to them," says Dr. Seligman.

> *"Caring about others, leaving an impact on people, brings happiness. When you carry out acts of kindness you get a wonderful feeling inside. It is as though something inside your body responds and says, yes, this is how I ought to feel."*
>
> – Harold Kushner, author of *When Bad Things Happen to Good People*

Existentialists believe it's the individual, not society, who's responsible for giving meaning to life and living it passionately. If you want to be happy, go out there and get it!

Buddhist monks, like the Dalai Lama, might advise that happiness is silence, meditation and offering unconditional compassion to others. I've learned in meditation that silence teaches the value of the moment, and that every moment brings opportunities; opportunities to appreciate each new and unique moment. For me, it's kind of a circle of happiness.

How do we get happy? I had many conversations with happiness experts, but three stood out:

Christopher Peterson was a professor of psychology at the University of Michigan. He was noted for his work in the study of optimism, health, character and well-being, and was one of the founders of "positive psychology." I talked to Chris before he passed away in October of 2012, and saved his words for this book. "The key to happiness seems to be giving," he said. "Giving makes you feel good about yourself. It puts meaning in your life. You have a sense of purpose because you matter to someone else."

Sonya Lyubomirsky's papers (University of California) were the first I reviewed years ago, and a key point stuck in my brain: up to 40% of our happiness might stem from those intentional cognitive, motivational and behavioral activities that we choose to engage in. Lyubomirsky wrote that happiness seekers should find new activities to become engaged in, preferably activities that *fit their values and interests*. Remember this, because later in the book we'll use our values, skills and talents to do just that.

Richard Leider leads AARP's *Life Reimagined* initiative. Leider says the essentials for happiness and well-being include these three Ms:

1. Money – resources to obtain basic needs
2. Medicine – health and activity
3. Meaning – friends and family, personal interests, such as hobbies and travel; making things better for others, such as volunteering, community service, helping the environment, or using your abilities to accomplish things that matter.

Of the third M, Leider says, "Meaning is essential for happiness and well-being."

Unhappy? Why?

A poll asked 100 people (50+ years old, employed or retired) when they were most unhappy. The results were:

56%   When I have unresolved conflict with others.
32%   When I feel inertia – not using my skills/talents to give/create/move forward.
12%   When I see the money's running out.

An interpretation of these results:

First, we want to have healthy relationships, but after that, we want to ensure we're using our natural and learned skills and talents. I'm sure you've considered this unused feeling before: *I feel untapped. I want to use the skills I'm good at. I want to feel valued and fulfilled!* So, the second key to being happy (after great relationships) may be to use what Dr. Seligman calls your "signature strengths." We want to find opportunities to use our strengths for something of meaning, something a little bigger than us.

Does Money = Happiness?

In our society, we're taught that happiness comes when we "have it all," like friends, family, prestige, influence, clothes, cars and other toys. But, there are many stories of that affluence creating its own dissatisfaction, like boredom, disenchantment, obesity, drug addiction, alcoholism, etc. Research has shown that wealthy people are generally no happier than the rest of us. Now, that doesn't mean I don't want to be very rich because, well, you know, I could handle it.

In experiments done by Lyubomirsky, she noted that how people spend their money may be as important as how much money they earn. Spending money on others might represent a more effective route to happiness than spending money on oneself. By the way, we're going to deal with your resources, like money, real estate, etc. and their place in legacy-building, later in the book.

> "Happiness lies not in the mere possession of money; it lies in the joy of achievement, in the thrill of creative effort."
>
> – Franklin D. Roosevelt

3. The Connection Between Legacy and Happiness?

Let's remind ourselves of our definition:

A legacy is something I create that connects and enhances lives now, and will continue to positively affect others when I'm gone.

Some key points we've learned about happiness are:

- Pursue activities that fit your values and have meaning.
- Use your abilities – skills, talents.
- Give to others.
- Be proactive – *Go do it!*

Dr. Seligman is the author of over 20 books on happiness. He says there are three components to happiness. I believe each component has a foot in legacy:

Pleasure: This is a short-term positive emotion, which gives us feelings like warmth, comfort and rapture. Try sex, your favorite pizza, relaxing, socializing, exercising, watching TV, playing with the kids, etc. Building each legacy gives pleasure too. It just feels good to create them and see their effect.

Engagement: Shows the depth of involvement in what you're doing; it's how deeply you're in the flow. This can happen when you're at work, during romance, while practicing a hobby, etc. When you're really engaged and happy, there's a virtual stopping of time and a loss of self-consciousness during that absorbing activity. You are immersed, one with the music. Engagement in legacy means being connected with family and friends, and especially new friends.

Meaning: Dr. Seligman says you create meaning when you use your signature strengths in the service of something that you believe is larger than you are. "We build our lives around pursuing pleasure. It turns out that engagement and meaning are much more important." Seligman's biggest recommendation? Know what your signature strengths are. "We can become lastingly happier by using our signature strengths more often and in new ways." This is the key to legacy-building: *using your signature strengths for something you believe in.*

So, to create some new legacies (and the happiness that comes with them) you need to:

- Know what your deeply held values are.
- Be aware of your skills, talents and strengths (and new ones you want to acquire).
- Be willing to create and give what is valuable, meaningful and fun.
- Be ready to connect with more people through meaningful relationships.

Your intentional legacies, created with your values, skills and talents (your signature strengths), can create happiness for you, your family, your future family, your friends, your community, country and world.

Philosopher Bertrand Russell said in *The Conquest of Happiness*:

"Happiness is not, except in very rare cases, something that drops into the mouth, like a ripe fruit. Happiness must be, for most men and women, an achievement rather than a gift of the gods, and in this achievement, effort, both inward and outward, must play a great part."

Once you've created your next legacy, look in the mirror. See the look? That's what I call your Legacy Smile.

Are you happy? There are dozens of online sites with questionnaires that will score your level of happiness, all for free. You'll find some of them in our FREE download of *The Legacy Starter* at www.createmylegacy.com. If you're curious to see the wisdom of 100 happiness professors from around the world, you'll see a selection of the keys to happiness from Leo Bormans' *The World Book of Happiness* here too.

Happy, yes. But, as you enhance yours and other's lives with your new legacies, do you need to have your name on the side of a building, or a statue of yourself in the park? Do legacy builders want their ego stroked? There have been some, and there may be others. But you? Let's look at legacy and the ego.

Ego – Hey, look what I did!

"Don't talk about yourself.
That will be done when you leave."

– Wilson Mizner, American playwright

Do you need a big ego to think about legacy?

A couple of years ago my wife and I toured Egypt. If there is a place on earth where those who have gone before us are shouting, "Hey, look what I did!", it's Egypt. The pyramids, tombs and temples were built to honor the achievements of their builders. The walls of hieroglyphics tell the stories of their conquests, and will do so for thousands of years. Egypt is "look at me" writ big.

Take good ol' Ramesses II. He was the third Egyptian pharaoh who reigned 1279 BC – 1213 BC. He is often regarded as the greatest, most celebrated and powerful pharaoh of the Egyptian Empire. He brought peace, maintained Egyptian borders, and built great and numerous monuments to himself across the empire. After reigning for 30 years, Ramesses joined a selected group of Egypt's longest-lived kings and celebrated a jubilee called the Sed Festival, during which the king was ritually transformed into a god.

In 1255 BC, Ramesses and his queen, Nefertari, traveled to Nubia to inaugurate a new temple, the great Abu Simbel. There sit giant and lasting monuments of Ramesses and his queen, "egos cast in stone," as he affirmed his role as Egypt's greatest pharaoh.

Ego? Sure. But he influenced Egypt for thousands of years. And he still does as we tell others to roam the Nile and visit his Abu Simbel. Ramesses died at about 90 years of age from severe dental problems, arthritis and hardening of the arteries. When his mummy was exhumed from the Valley of the Kings and taken to Paris for examination in 1974, Ramesses II was issued an Egyptian passport that listed his occupation as "King (deceased)." They discovered that his head was kept on with a piece of wood lodged in his upper chest. It's believed that during the mummification process his head was accidentally knocked off. I guess even those with great legacies can have the occasional migraine.

Another long-term idea to consider, this from my friend and author, Rick Antonson:

Cathedral Thinking

The concept of Cathedral Thinking stretches back to medieval times when construction began on the soaring, cavernous and magnificent cathedrals that served as places of worship, community gathering spaces and safe havens. They still dot Europe's landscape. It was the individual architects, stone masons and carpenters who built those cathedrals, yet never saw the culmination of their efforts. But they shared one purpose: to create a lasting legacy that would be an inspiration to others, long after they left this earth. They added their part to a vision of something that would be bigger than themselves.

Cathedral Thinking has been applied to space exploration, city planning and other long-term goals that require decades of foresight and planning so future generations can enjoy their full realization. They all require the same foundation: a far-reaching vision, a well thought-out blueprint and a commitment to enhance other people's lives in the future. As you learn in this book what your legacies can be, and you confirm that yes, you'd like to leave something behind to enhance other people's lives, does this mean you're egocentric? Methinks not. You're just practicing Cathedral Thinking.

I know some rich people, people whose names are on the sides of buildings, hospital wings or university libraries, who have made exceptional amounts of money. Their names are there to be recognized for their donation and the good that it will produce. Do they have big egos? Do they see themselves as masters of the universe, wrapped up in their own importance? If they do (and most don't), that's fine by me. It's been a fair trade, I think, as the story of their legacy's value will carry on for hundreds of years, along with their name.

> *"Do all the good you can, and make as little fuss about it as possible."*
>
> – Charles Dickens

I've worked with successful people, quiet philanthropists, who are as humble as the day they were born. They too are intent on creating lasting legacies. But their name, their ego, is less out there. They have a different need for recognition.

What differentiates humans from other species is transcendent dimension; our ability to go beyond the limits of normal experience and thinking. To dream and build and project the future we want to be a part of. Maybe ego is part of transcendence, a search for meaning now, and a way to achieve immortality.

I think we all have a need for some recognition. You may have had the experience at a birthday, anniversary or retirement party where your friends and family toast you, salute your strengths, your stories and maybe your foibles. Yes, it feels good to be recognized, to know that they've noticed, to feel that what you've done has been noticed.

When your final recognition is read, your eulogy, wouldn't you love to hear the hallmarks of your life and the legacies you left behind. You would smile. *Yup, I did that, and that, and that. And I'm leaving these for you.* If that's ego, so be it. We are connecting with a longing to be recognized. It's natural to want to feel, *I was here. I mattered.*

In a few chapters, we'll be getting into two of the three main types of legacy: your story and the stories of your family and friends. Think for a minute about this. If you had the stories of the lives of your great, great-grandparents, stories of how they lived, what their joys and challenges were, what they thought of the future, would that be interesting? I think there's something hugely intriguing about even the most meager details about our ancestors. If they spent the time to collect their stories, knowing they'll be read by you hundreds of years later, is that ego? It was their gift of connection with us, their future generations, who are tied by blood. The stories of their lives might have seemed mundane to them, but I think we'd be fascinated. And so it is when we collect our stories for our descendants. They'll be fascinated by how we lived.

If your vision of immortality is to be a statue of yourself, that's fine. But your ego will have to be aware of the pigeons. What we will begin to learn now is how to weave ourselves into the lives of others, those who will enjoy our transcendent cathedrals, our legacies.

So, does legacy = ego? Probably not. But as one man in a seminar told me, "I don't want to be noticed. I do want to be remembered though."

"What you leave behind is not what is engraved in stone monuments, but what is woven into the lives of others."

– Pericles,
General of Athens
in its Golden Age

Now, if you were raised with one of the world's great religions, do you remember being taught anything about legacy? Can't say that I knelt as an altar boy on those oh-so-hard marble steps with legacy on my mind. Yet within all those religions, it's there. You just have to look!

Religion – It Glitters Like Gold!

"You've got to do unto others
Like you'd have them
Like you'd have them
Do unto you."

– Bob Dylan, *Do Right to Me Baby*

My Religious Story

I was raised as a Catholic. I was an altar boy, a choirboy, and a boy scout selling Christmas trees with frozen hands on those freezing December evenings to benefit the church. For a while I thought Father Robb is what I would become. Me, a Catholic priest! Who'da thought?

Each morning, in grades 3 to 6, I would trudge through the snow to St. Mary's Cathedral, about a mile and a half from our home. I would go because I wanted to serve mass, even though I wasn't scheduled to. If one of the other boys didn't show up, I was in! This enthusiasm to kneel on those marble altar steps for an hour at a time, and breathe in that thick incense smoke, gained me many points with Monsignor Smith and the other priests. I had a lock on a good room in heaven.

It all ended in grade 7. At 13, a boy starts to notice other things, and is rather easily distracted. What held my attention, what really caused me to stare and have thoughts that would surely cause God to ban me from entering the pearly gates, was Maria.

Now, Maria was only 13 too, a nice Italian girl. She was beautiful, and had, well, a more mature body than some of the other girls. At this stage of my life, I have to admit, I wasn't thinking legacy. All through grade 7 all I dreamt about was having a family with Maria. But alas, it wasn't to be. On the first day of grade 8 I found out Maria's family had moved to San Francisco. She hadn't called to say goodbye. She probably thought I got the strap too often.

My altar boy career ended and other priorities took over, like sports and gaining favors from girls who weren't going to move away. Still, my brush with religion stayed with me. Through the rest of my schooling, at university, and with life's gathered experience, I learned a little about the world's religions, how they had shaped the world, and continue to.

Legacy and Religion?

Do each of the world's great religions speak of the concept of legacy? Do these religions talk about creating and leaving something behind to enhance the lives of those who follow us? I wonder if there is a common teaching about legacy in:

- Taoism and its Tao Te Ching;
- Sikhism and its religious text Guru Granth Sahib Ji;
- Buddhism's *The Path to Enlightenment*;
- Islam's Qur'an;
- Hinduism's four aims: Dharma, Artha, Kama and Moksha;
- Judaism's Torah;
- Christianity's Bible.

I thought that in this panoply of religious beliefs that encircle our world there would be one shared belief, one common teaching that paralleled our idea of legacy.

As I looked for that common teaching, I kept seeing gold.

Gold has symbolized the imperishable. Like our friend Tut in Egypt and his other kingly friends, many are encased in gold to symbolize eternal life. In temples and houses of worship of various religions, gold is often prominent, representing the pure, eternal and incorruptible truths that are believed to be embodied there. One example is the Golden Temple in Amritsar, India.

My wife and I were recently in the São Francisco Church and Convent in Salvador, Bahia, Brazil. I was awestruck at the interior, which was covered in 250 lbs. (100 kg.) of gold leaf.

> *"There are realms of gold hidden deep in the human heart"*
>
> – Hindu proverb

The Buddha is frequently portrayed in gold. One of the most impressive examples is the huge image of the Buddha found in the Wat Traimit in Bangkok, Thailand, an image made entirely of gold. Throughout the world gold is associated with heaven.

Gold is a metaphor for the best of all things human. You know these familiar phrases:

- As good as *gold.*
- A heart of *gold.*
- Worth her weight in *gold.*
- Going for the *gold.*
- I struck *gold.*
- Everything he touches turns to *gold.*
- It glitters like *gold.*

Gold symbolizes illumination, light and even spiritual enlightenment. I uncovered phrases that had a common theme, like this one written in Egypt, 1650 BC: "Do for one who may do for you that you may cause him thus to do."

And finally, Mahatma Gandhi brought gold, religion and legacy together: "He who seeks truth alone follows the golden rule."

Finally, the Rule. The Golden Rule!

That's it. The golden rule! The most universal, consistent and prevalent moral principle in history: "Do unto others as I would have them do unto me."

"The golden rule doesn't specifically cover legacy and all religions," said Paul McKenna, creator of the Golden Rule Poster, "but this does a lot of work, real fast. Religions sometimes don't agree on a lot, but the golden rule is a common meeting place. And it fits with legacy."

The golden rule is infused with legacy. I'll feel good (and be happier) knowing my legacies will enhance other lives. Those who receive my legacies will pay it forward again… and again. I will start a domino effect of legacy creation.

The golden rule is also known as the Law of Reciprocity. It's part of our planet's common language, shared by people with differing but overlapping conceptions of morality, and by all their religions.

Thanks to McKenna of www.scarboromissions.ca for the following table. Contact him for a poster that tells the same story.

Religion	Golden Rule Expression
BAHA'I FAITH	Lay not on any soul a load that you would not wish to be laid upon you, and desire not for anyone the things you would not desire for yourself.
BUDDHISM	Treat not others in ways that you yourself would find hurtful.
CHRISTIANITY	In everything, do to others as you would have them do to you; for this is the law and the prophets.
CONFUCIANISM	One phrase that sums up the basis of all good conduct...loving kindness. Or, do not do to others what you do not want done to yourself.
HINDUISM	This is the sum of duty: do not do to others what would cause pain if done to you.
ISLAM	Not one of you truly believes until you wish for others what you wish for yourself.
JAINISM	One should treat all creatures in the world as one would like to be treated.
JUDAISM	What is hateful to you, do not do to your neighbor. This is the whole Torah; all the rest is commentary.
NATIVE SPIRITUALITY	We are as much alive as we keep the earth alive.
SIKHISM	I am a stranger to no one; and no one is a stranger to me. Indeed, I am a friend to all.
TAOISM	Regard your neighbor's gain as your own, and your neighbor's loss as your own.
UNITARIANISM	We affirm respect for the interdependent web of all existence of which we are a part.
ZOROASTRIANISM	Do not do unto others whatever is injurious to yourself.

In these sceptical-about-our-leaders days, it's good to know the golden rule once had a tryout in politics. American President Millard Fillmore (1800–1874) tried to begin a golden rule legacy when he said, "We should act toward other nations as we wish them to act toward us." Maybe this should be printed in big, bold letters above the Secretary-General's chair at the United Nations.

And so it is with people. As we create, they will create. As Desmond Tutu said, "We're made for goodness."

. . . .

I worked in Hong Kong for a few years, producing the multimedia content in their Museum of History. One day, the curator took me out to lunch and, without speaking it, reminded me again of the joy of giving. As we were about to leave he gave me a package.

"For you," he said with a broad smile. He knew I collected masks, and sure enough it was a small replica of an ancient mask. I knew it would be valuable and possess a great story. I was very touched, and it showed.

"You didn't have to," I muttered.

He smiled and said that it was his pleasure, and then quoted this ancient Chinese proverb: "A little fragrance always clings to the hand that gives the rose."

This was our small lunchtime example of the golden rule. He knew that if he gave, he would surely receive.

. . . .

It's kind of comforting to know that every human being on the planet who has ever been touched by any religion, may have deep in their heart a version of the golden rule. Do unto others as you would have them do unto you. Give and you will receive. As you begin to create your legacies, so will others see them, benefit from them and want to create their own to affect others. So, knowing your version of the golden rule will be the first domino of your rose-scented legacies.

What will you create your legacies with? You'll build them with your raw materials – your unique values, skills and talents (your signature strengths). You're not exactly sure what they are? Well, the next chapter will help you identify and assemble those raw materials so you can lay down the foundation for all your legacies.

Values
Skills
Talents
Compassion
Achievement
Challenge
Teacher
Opportunity
Farmer
Gardener
Counselor
Writer
Cook
Musician
Card Player

Your Raw Materials – Values, Skills, Talents

"Happiness is that state of consciousness which proceeds from the achievement of one's values."

– Ayn Rand

Let's define the raw materials of legacy-building so you know what you're working with: your values, skills and talents. Soon, you'll put them to work, but for now, let's clarify what they are.

Your Values

I'll bet you haven't considered this too often: *What rules do you live your life by?* Most of us have to think hard to find the answer to this important and, yes, fairly tough question. What tenets are you living by that give your life purpose and meaning? What are those elements that govern your life and give it rules? What values do you want to salute as you build your legacies?

Below is a list of values. Have a look at them, slowly. When one catches your attention, circle it or write it down. It's either part of your life, or you want it to be. Take your time and when you're done, I'll tell you what my top 10 are.

. . . .

Accomplishment, Achievement, Acknowledgment, Adventure, Affluence, Ambition, Appreciation, Assertiveness, Balance, Beauty, Belonging, Bravery, Calmness, Candor, Care, Challenge, Charity, Cheerfulness, Clarity, Cleverness, Commitment, Community, Compassion, Competence, Competition, Conformity, Connection, Conservation, Contribution, Control, Cooperation, Courage, Creativity, Curiosity, Decisiveness, Determination, Devotion, Dignity, Diligence, Drive, Education, Efficiency, Empathy, Encouragement, Endurance, Entertainment, Environmentalism, Experience, Exuberance, Fairness, Faith, Fearlessness, Financial Independence, Fitness, Flexibility, Fortitude, Freedom, Friendliness, Generosity, Grace, Growth, Happiness, Health, Honesty, Humility, Humor, Imagination, Independence, Inspiration, Integrity, Intelligence, Joy, Kindness, Knowledge, Leadership, Love, Loyalty, Making a Difference, Meaning, Mindfulness, Modesty, Nature, Open-Mindedness, Opportunity, Optimism, Outdoors, Passion, Patience, Peace, Perceptiveness, Perseverance, Philanthropy, Playfulness, Pleasure, Pragmatism, Precision, Professionalism, Prosperity, Rationality, Recognition, Reflection, Reputation, Resourcefulness, Respect, Responsibility, Self-Reliance, Sensitivity, Sincerity, Spirituality, Spontaneity, Success, Synergy, Teaching, Teamwork, Tranquility, Trust, Truth, Uniqueness, Valor, Vision, Warmth, Wealth, Winning, Wisdom

. . . .

Well done. You might have circled three… or 23.

This simple exercise is hugely important because legacy creation always has a value tied to it. Oh, my top 10 values?

1. Integrity
2. Connection
3. Wisdom
4. Creativity
5. Joy
6. Health
7. Opportunity
8. Adventure
9. Contribution
10. Freedom

In the charity work I've done, the values that drove me were Contribution and Connection. When I got cancer, Health became #1. Six years clear now, I've moved it to #6. It's these values that I check in with when there are some decisions to make.

So, what are the values you lead your life by? From those values you circled, pick what you think are up to 10 of the most important values and write them down here:

1. _____
2. _____
3. _____
4. _____
5. _____

6. _____
7. _____
8. _____
9. _____
10. _____

These are the values you'll use to build powerful and memorable legacies. And if you don't think you've really nailed all your values just yet, you'll also have over 500 values to choose from in the free download that comes with this book.

Your Skills and Talents

Not only are values important in legacy-building, but so are your skills and talents because those traits make you, *you*. It's these unique traits that will allow you to create some unique legacies. We'll go over this in more detail in future chapters, but let's agree on a couple of ideas first.

A skill, as opposed to a talent, is what you work with; it can also be used to make a living. It's used at work, almost daily and ideally, this skill improves as you use it. Knowing your skills could answer the questions: *What do you have to know to make a living? What do you consider yourself an expert in?*

Here's a short list of skills. Add others that are important to you.

Accounting, Acting, Administration, Advertising, Arborist, Audio Engineering, Baking, Banking, Biologist, Building, Carpentry, Child Psychology, Chiropractic, Comedian, Computer Programming, Cooking, Counseling, Dentistry, Doctor, Editing, Electrician, Electronics, Engineering, Farming, Fashion Design, Finance Specialist, Foreign Language Teaching, Gardening, Geologist, Graphic Design, Health Specialist, Human Resources, Illustration, Innovator, Interior Design, Interpreter, Jeweler, Journalist, Landscape Design, Lawyer, Leadership Teacher, Librarian, Marketing, Mathematician, Media Production, Meeting Manager, Musician, Negotiating, Networking, Opera Singing, Organizing, Painting, Physiotherapy, Planning, Plumbing, Public Relations, Public Speaking, Researching, Retail, Sales, Software Programming, Teaching, Training, Truck Driver, Veterinary, Video Production, Website Building, Welding, Writing

_____   _____   _____   _____

Here are my three skills from this list:

1. Media Production   2. Marketing   3. Public Speaking

Your three skills:

1. _____   2. _____   3. _____

Well done! Now, a talent is what you play with. It's like you were born with this talent. You probably don't make a living with it. It's a hobby that you practice for enjoyment. And you're pretty good at it. Knowing your talents will answer the question: *What do you do for fun?*

Here's a short list of talents. Add others that are important to you.

Acting, Artist, Astrology, Athletics, Checkers, Cheerleading, Chess, Choir Directing, Computer Programming, Cooking, Creative Thinking, Crosswords, Dancing, Debating, Entertaining, Fishing, Fitness Coaching, Games Player, Gardening, Golf, Hunting, Inventor, Juggling, Knitting, Lifeguard, Listening, Magician, Mechanic, Mediation, Mountain Climbing, Musician, Numerology, Outdoor Enthusiast, People Connector, Photography, Poetry, Public Speaking, Sculpture/Ceramics, Sewing/Quilting, Singing, Speed Reading, Sports Coaching, Story Collecting, Storytelling, Swimming, Video Gaming, Woodworking, Writing, Yoga Enthusiast

_____   _____   _____   _____

Here are my three talents from this list:

1. Gardening   2. Writing   3. Outdoor Enthusiast

Your three talents:

1. _____   2. _____   3. _____

Okay, we now have the raw materials, or signature strengths, of your legacy-building. They are the:

• Values you live by;
• Skills that make you valuable;
• Talents you enjoy.

If you haven't yet written down your values, skills and talents, I encourage you to do so. Whether you find this challenging or easy, I believe you'll be pleased to see them on paper. As an experiment, I sent the same list of values, skills and talents to friends and colleagues in my email list. Within a day, I had 75 replies from enthusiastic people who were eager to take a few moments and find out what their legacy raw materials were. Here are a few of them:

Cathy

Values:	Connection, Creativity, Kindness, Integrity, Curiosity
Skills:	Storytelling, Conceptualizing
Talents:	Cooking, Nature Lover, Collector

Alvin

Values:	Completeness, Connection, Compassion, Community, Health
Skills:	Vision, Consolidation, Team Building
Talents:	Traveling, Mellowing, Kayaking

Chuck

Values:	Cheerfulness, Contribution, Fairness, Honesty, Integrity
Skills:	Fairness Developer, Team Builder, Leader
Talents:	Handyman, Traveling, Reading

Dann

Values:	Optimism, Vision, Achievement, Humor, Compassion
Skills:	Marketing, Deal Making, People Management
Talents:	Sports, Chef, Organizing

Anna

Values:	Freedom, Health, Happiness, Success, Making a Difference
Skills:	Consulting, Teaching, Advising
Talents:	Designing, Dancing, Creating

Eddy

Values:	Achievement, Adventure, Teamwork, Passion, Humility
Skills:	Leadership, Marketing, Managing People
Talents:	Music, Reading, Photography

George

Values:	Curiosity, Pragmatism, Tolerance, Remembrance, Enthusiasm
Skills:	Media Production, Teaching, Cooking
Talents:	Music, Reading, Writing

In a few chapters, we'll be building real, live, enjoyable, connecting, happiness-creating legacies with your raw materials. But to give you an idea, here's one example taken from my list.

Wendy

Value:	Determination
Skill:	Problem Solving
Talent:	Biking

Wendy wants one of her legacies to be at-risk kids who become healthier and more focussed by learning competitive road biking (you know, the Tour de France kind). She's working with the police and three bike shops in her city to resurrect stolen bikes. Donations have helped buy clip-on bike shoes and helmets. Wendy teaches a garage-classroom session on safety, and then leads kids on their first one-hour peddle on a quiet road. They're now beginning to race among themselves. About 100 kids are involved and the group is growing quickly. The kids began to work and save for their own bikes. One day, the story will be told of a Wendy graduate winning their first big race.

People are learning of Wendy's bikers because it's a great story. It's the story of your legacies that people will enjoy telling. It's the story that will ensure your legacy lives on, and that you'll be remembered.

So, what's a story?

LEGACY AND STORY

So, what's a story?

"Tell me a fact and I'll learn.
Tell me a truth and I'll believe.
Tell me a story and it will live in my heart forever."

– Aboriginal proverb

Legacy is all about story… stories proudly told now, and after you're gone. Your legacies will connect you with people, make you happier and affect other people's lives. And no matter how big or small those legacies are, each one will tell a story, ensuring that legacy lives on.

Next chapter, you're going to build a new and simple legacy, and its story. But for a moment, enjoy a classic example of a memorable story that has lasted for millenniums.

Raven Steals the Light

Many years ago, the earth was covered by inky darkness, making it difficult for anyone to hunt or fish or gather berries. An old man lived in a hut along the banks of a stream with his daughter, but he didn't know if she was beautiful or homely because it was dark. It was dark because the old man kept all the light in the universe in a box, and stored that box in several other boxes. It was his hidden treasure.

Mischievous Raven wasn't happy because he blundered about in the dark bumping into everything. One day he heard the old man muttering about the light and his boxes. Raven decided to steal the light, but he had to find a way to get inside the hut.

Each day, the young girl would go to the stream to fetch water. Raven transformed himself into a tiny hemlock needle and floated into the girl's bucket. With his trickster magic, he made the girl thirsty and, as she took a drink, he slipped down her throat. Once down in her warm insides he changed again, this time into a small human being.

The girl didn't know what was happening to her. One day Raven emerged as a little boy child. Both father and daughter were delighted with their new addition. As the Raven child explored his new surroundings, he soon determined that the light must be in the big box in the corner. When he first tried to open the box, his grandfather scolded him profusely, so the boy cried and squawked even more. The grandfather caved in and gave the child the biggest box to play with. This brought peace for a brief time, but it wasn't long before the Raven child cried again, and the grandfather gave him the next box, and the next, until finally only one box remained.

The old man agreed to let the raven child play with the light for only a moment. As he tossed the ball of light, the child changed back into Raven. He quickly snatched the light in his beak and flew through the smoke hole into the sky. The world changed forever. The sky was bright. There were mountains and forests and their reflections danced on the rivers and oceans.

Far away though, Eagle was awakened and he launched skyward. He was curious and wanted the light too. His target was now clearly in sight.

Raven was so excited about his newly revealed world that he nearly didn't see Eagle bearing down on him. Swerving sharply to escape Eagle's outstretched talons, Raven dropped nearly half of the ball of light, and it fell to earth. It shattered into one large and many small pieces, but they bounced back up into the heavens where they remain to this day as the moon and the stars.

Eagle pursued Raven beyond the rim of the world. Raven was exhausted by the long chase, and let go of what light he still had. The light floated gracefully above the clouds, and became the sun rising up over the mountains to the east.

The first rays of the morning sun brought light through the smoke hole of the old man's house. He was weeping in sorrow over his great loss. However, he looked up and saw his daughter for the first time. She was more beautiful than he could have imagined.

I am reminded of this story every time I pass by my Raven Steals the Light mask hanging in our home. This story is one of thousands of North American aboriginal stories as told by the Inuit of the Arctic to the Seminole of Florida. Indigenous storytelling is meant to teach, heal, reflect and honor all life, as well as our human ancestors. Oftentimes, these stories are about the animals of the storyteller's homeland; the coyote of the desert, the buffalo of the Plains, the beaver of the Eastern woodlands, and in my world, the raven, eagle, whale and salmon of the Pacific Northwest. Most importantly, these stories have survived for generations without our technology to keep them alive.

And that's what story is about! The stories of your legacies will keep your legacies alive. Those stories will communicate your legacy's truths and benefits, and others will be moved to tell the story, again and again. This way your legacies will live on. This way you'll be remembered.

From The International Storytelling Center at www.storytellingcenter.net:

"After years of scientific research in 17 different fields, analysts conclude that storytelling is our most powerful tool for effective communication."

When Did Storytelling Begin?

Storytelling might have begun with Grog as he arrived home to the cave one night, disheveled, bleeding and empty-handed. He speaks to his wife:

"I club mastodon. He look at me, mad, like saying, 'You hit me?' I club again. 'Me hungry,' I say. He pick me up with big horn. I poke stick in eye. He ROAR and throw me to ground. He rise up on back feet, ready to crush me. I go left! I go right! I club his foot... and run! So, no dinner tonight. Sorry honey."

The 35,000-year-old paintings on the walls of the Lascaux Caves in France are our earliest recorded evidence of storytelling. Maybe Grog went on to study graphic design?

In *The World of Storytelling*, Anne Pellowski says storytelling grew out of the need to be playful, to explain the physical world, to honor supernatural forces and to communicate experience.

One of our oldest-surviving records is found in the Egyptian Westcar Papyrus in which the sons of Cheops (the pyramid builder) entertained their father with stories. The epic tale, *Gilgamesh*, which relays the story of a Sumerian king, is frequently cited in history texts as our oldest-surviving epic tale, written over 4,000 years ago.

The Greeks, Romans and Gypsies' nomadic existence carried tales far and wide. Medieval troubadours told stories as a means of bringing together the lives of people, creating a sense of community and shared understanding. Records of storytelling have been found in many languages, including Sanskrit, Old German, Latin, Chinese, Greek, Latin, Icelandic and Old Slavonic.

Stories throughout history come in all shapes and sizes, such as myths, legends, tall tales, fairy tales, fables, folk tales, parables and epic adventures. These stories were told, retold and passed down from father to son, mother to daughter and from one generation to another. Great teachers, like Homer and Plato, Jesus and Gandhi used stories to instruct and illustrate.

For thousands of years storytelling was used to explain significant events like storms, tidal waves, lightning and fire. Stories of gods were used to bind individuals to common belief systems, and moral tales explained laws to help ensure some cooperation in society.

This was all oral storytelling. After the invention of the printing press in 1450, stories became more available in print, hence our bookshelves are filled with William Shakespeare, Danielle Steel, Harold Robbins, Dr. Seuss and J.K. Rowling. By the way, did you know Gutenberg's bibles sold at the 1455 Frankfurt Book Fair for an equivalent of three years' pay for the average clerk? Today, Gutenberg would be in the eBook business.

Storytelling Today?

Today, stories are everywhere, in every society and culture, because storytelling is in our DNA. To tell stories is to be human. Stories are told to entertain, teach, pass on knowledge and wisdom. They define our values, our dreams, and sometimes, our prejudices and hatreds.

> "Stories have to be told or they die. And when they die, we can't remember who we are or why we're here."
>
> – Sue Monk Kidd, author of *The Secret Life of Bees*

Stories are told in the media, through music, books, movies and news. They can influence us in many ways, like when the advertising industry uses stories to brand their products with emotion and facts that are intended to open your mind, heart, tear ducts and wallet.

The Lascaux Caves would have been fascinating to find, to wonder what those images were meant to tell us. But, they don't hold a burning, storytelling torch to the method that most of us will learn about them from – the Internet. In your hands or on your giant TV screen, stories fly around the world in seconds. Like it or not, the Internet has created millions of storytellers (see YouTube), some brilliant, some rich, some gawdawful.

Perhaps this turn toward storytelling in society is our attempt to better communicate with each other? We know from millions of years of doing it that telling stories to each other will connect us better than anything else. Technology may race ahead, but the human spirit still deeply yearns for a sense of human connection. The legacies you begin here will create new and lasting connections.

Let's begin to build your legacies. You remember our definition:

A legacy is something I create that connects and enhances lives now, and will continue to positively affect others when I'm gone.

Your legacies will give you happiness while you live, and they will give your life meaning when you're gone. They will be powerful, simple and true. We will build your legacies using three methods:

1. TELL your story
2. GATHER their stories
3. CREATE new stories

1. TELL Your Story

Dan McAdams argues in his book, *The Redemptive Self*, that people give meaning and unity to their lives by developing life stories that define who they are. I believe the greatest gift you could give your family, those who care for you, and those who follow generations from now, will be the story of who you are. Half of a printed page or a two-hour video, you decide. Said screenwriter, Antwone Fisher, "Don't pass through life without leaving something behind for others to learn from your experience. You may discover a you you've never known." In the next section, "Legacy 1: TELL Your Story," you'll be shown how to get ready. And yes, you have a story to tell!

2. GATHER Their Stories

I didn't want my father's story to go with him, so I "gathered" it. In this chapter you'll learn the simple techniques to ensure the stories, wisdom, experience and philosophy of people important to you don't disappear. If they go without their story being told it's, "Like a library burning," says Scott Farnsworth in his book of the same name. All those stories, and all that wisdom, gone! Gathering their stories will be your legacy that allows your descendants to smile and appreciate the lives we led. Your legacy will be that your descendants know who they came from. We'll do this in "Legacy 2: GATHER Their Stories".

3. CREATE New Stories

I heard this often in my seminars: "I don't know where to start. I don't know what my legacies can be." Here's what I know: whoever you are, whatever you've done with your life, you have the values, skills, talents and resources to create tens, hundreds or thousands of legacies, from tiny to tremendous. They will make you happy and enhance lives, now and later. In the section, "Legacy 3: CREATE New Stories", you'll learn how to build those new legacies, those new stories of your life.

Learning these three methods of legacy-building will help you decide what you want your legacies to be, how to create them and the stories that arise from them. You'll have a very clear perspective, for the rest of your life, on what a legacy is and how to use these new skills to deliberately create one.

So, let's build your first powerful legacy, your memorable story, the story of *you!*

Legacy 1: TELL Your Story

A young boy went to his grandfather and asked,
   "Grandfather, is it true that the lion is the king of the jungle?"
   "Yes," said the old man, "but why do you ask?"
   "Well," said the boy, "in all the stories that I've read and heard, man will always defeat the lion. So, how can this be true?"
   The old man looked his grandson in the eyes. "It will always be that way, my son, until the lion tells the story."

You are the lion. In this chapter you will learn to roar.
In a nice way.

This is about *your* story, told by *you*. And, if your brain just told you, *I don't have a story to tell*, that's an impossibility. It's impossible because you are a unique human with a unique story. In a couple of minutes you're going to have the first outline of your story in front of you. It's time the world heard about the lion, from the lion. You will be happier, you'll know yourself better, and will be proud to tell people in the future what really made you tick.

John Kotre says generativity, "is this feeling of mattering, of creating lasting value, of passing your very self on to others." But what is "passing of your very self?" As you read earlier, 77% of Boomers and their parents agreed that the sharing of values and life's lessons is a priority. I have a feeling that as Boomers pass values and lessons along, and then move forward, Generation Xs will think it is equally important to pass on their values and life's lessons to Generation Ys, and then, well, you get the idea.

Most people would have some difficulty if they were asked to write their story. But, we're going to make this easy, even illuminating. The skeletal structure of this story, and the meat we'll put in it, will be our values.

The Story of Your Values

Values dictate how you interact with others and how you manage your personal life. They influence decision-making. Psychotherapist Carl Jung asks, "What is the myth that is managing your life?" Most of us aren't very conscious of the internal myth or story that is the source of every thought, emotion or relationship in our life.

When we're clearer on what our values are, when we connect with the stories of those values, a funny thing happens – we start to live up to them. Seeing them on paper can make us happier. Yet, most of us don't spend a lot of time thinking about them. Until now.

You may have picked your five most important values from the chapter "Raw Materials," but if you haven't, please do that now. There's also a list of about 500 values in the free download at www.createmylegacy.com. Select the top five values that you think are some of the values that run your life. Yes, you have more than five, and you can change them later. But let's begin with five.

Because we're doing this together, here are my top five values:

1. Integrity   3. Wisdom   5. Joy
2. Connection   4. Creativity

Your top five values:

1. _____   2. _____   3. _____

        4. _____   5. _____

We're ready to document our unique story. If we don't put down even this brief story, one day it'll be gone forever, consigned to the trash heap of history. But let's learn a bit more first.

The Ethical Will/Legacy Letter

What you're going to create with your values is sometimes called an ethical will, or a Legacy Letter. It isn't a legal will, and you won't need a lawyer. This is just one way to tell your story.

Legal wills bequeath valuables, they say who gets what. An ethical will or Legacy Letter (LL) gives value to the "ethics of your life" that you want to pass on so those who follow you can benefit from your wisdom.

The Hebrew Bible first described LLs 3,000 years ago in Genesis, Chapter 49, where Jacob gathered his 12 sons around his deathbed. The tradition is also found in the Christian Bible [John, 15-18] and in many other cultures. Older LLs contained burial instructions, blessings and personal values of the writer. LLs were originally given orally, and over time they became written documents. They also became an important role for women as there was a time when women were barred from writing a legal will or dispensing property.

An LL is usually written to your loved ones to express hope that you'll be remembered for your values, but it also can describe your goals, life lessons, forgiveness (given and asked for) and love to your family, friends and community. An LL is a way to leave behind what's most important to you, other than physical possessions. Many years from now your descendants will read your LL and have a better understanding of who you were and how you lived in your world. Can you imagine if you had this from your great, great, great-grandparents? Why not give it to your future generations?

> *"Think for example about how rooted, how connected, you'd feel if you knew from your great, great-grandparents' own words what immigration was like, what they'd given up, what their hopes and dreams for themselves and you, yet unborn were, their personal hardships of the crossing and settling, what they missed about the old and treasured about the new, what was required to negotiate the unknown country, what biases they faced as newcomers, what they valued most of that experience."*
>
> – Rachael Freed, www.life-legacies.com

The Legacy Letter: A Start

Dr. Barry K. Baines is a hospice medical director in Minneapolis. In 1990, his dad was dying of lung cancer and Baines asked him to write a letter describing what was important to him.

"Why do you want me to do that?" shrugged his father. "I'll think about it." A few weeks later a letter addressed to Baines and his sister arrived in the mail. This is an excerpt:

"A few words to express my feelings and thoughts while time is running out on me. Through the years, I've tried to take care of my family and give them some of the better things in life. I tried and succeeded in being able to give my children a good education. Although I was only a working man, many were the times I worked two jobs for the extra money so that the family could have a little bit more. I have always believed in honesty and advocated truthfulness. I cherish the family with all my heart. I always felt that I gave of myself to everyone in the family. The satisfaction and gratification that I received in return is in the accomplishments of my children. No father could be as proud as your father is of you."

This was an important letter for Baines, as a month later his father passed away. He found out his father had written letters to five other members of the family, all of whom treasure them still. It was their first experience with an LL.

Spin forward to 1997. Baines was associate medical director for a hospice program in the Twin Cities area. A patient, Dennis, was in his late 40s, and dying of pancreatic cancer. He had a wife and two kids, but felt his life was a failure. Dennis wasn't leaving his family many resources and felt his life had no impact. He told Baines he was suffering, spiritually, 10 out of 10.

Baines remembered his father's letter, and with a colleague's help, put together some short questions for Dennis that would allow him to write and bequeath his values to his family.

"He grabbed it like a drowning man would grab a life preserver," said Baines. A few days later, with his LL done, Dennis said the suffering was gone. The 10 was now a zero.

"We were awestruck," said Baines.

With those experiences, Baines wrote and published, *Ethical Wills: Putting Your Values on Paper*. The power of an LL was obvious to Baines, both for those near the end of life, and for all of us who are living productive lives, with no end in sight.

"One day yours will be read," he promises, "whether tomorrow or years from now."

Rachael Freed is a former English teacher and therapist in Minneapolis, and conducts workshops and retreats where people ask themselves: *How do I want to be remembered? What have I learned? What do I want to pass on?*

"You learn you have something to say, and you know that you can write it," says Freed. "It can be a one-page letter to the people you love. It can be that simple."

My First Legacy Letter

The great thing is, our values, wisdom, experience, love, joys, advice and stories don't fit well into boiler plate wills and estate planning documents. Your LL could be one page, or a hundred.

You may remember my top five values:

1. Integrity
2. Connection
3. Wisdom
4. Creativity
5. Joy

Your top five values again?

1. _____   2. _____   3. _____

          4. _____   5. _____

Now, for each of your five values, write down answers to these questions:

1. Why is this value important to me?
2. How does this value show up in my life?

The following is a preview of my Legacy Letter, based on my top five values. This isn't the whole LL, but it shows how I've approached it:

Integrity

I wrote my thoughts on the importance of completing what I said I'd do, and doing the right thing. I tell the story of climbing a very technical mountain after promising to deliver a keepsake to the summit for a friend who had just lost his wife. I was absolutely exhausted and ready to quit about 500 feet below the summit. If I didn't push through I'd look at myself as a failure without the character or grit to succeed. I got to the summit and cried, hard.

Connection

I tell of the importance of having other people in my life, hearing their stories, and listening to their wisdom and experience. But mostly I tell of how easy it is to connect because it's a natural human urge to connect. I tell stories of walking into places around the world when my wife might say, "We don't belong," and coming out with new friends.

Wisdom

I tell of my need when I was younger to impress others with my smarts, and finally learned it was a little boring, for them and for me. I figured out that quiet wisdom was more fulfilling, and tell a few stories of slowly, slowly feeling a little wiser, but never, never as wise as the next person. To get there, more questions must be asked; more listening must be done, more silence must be appreciated.

Creativity

This value is important because it's made me feel good throughout my life. I always loved looking at things… differently. As in photography, if you think you have the best picture, turn around 180 degrees for a possible better shot. I tell the story of the joy of writing my first newspaper article at 20 years of age while hitchhiking in the blazing heat of Australia's desert. That planted a seed that became my life's career.

Joy

Back to the Dalai Lama. We're here to be happy. I write that the older I get the more I know there is joy in everything. I can be an entertainer to give joy, and a silent receiver of it in a quiet place. Although I haven't always been successful, my goal has been to leave people feeling better, and smiling for having been with me. My father taught me that in his last year. He was talking of moving to a new care home to be with a friend. A nurse grabbed my arm and said, "Don't let him go!" She was crying. "He makes us all feel so good." I hope to have many additional years of giving and receiving joy.

Take each of your five values and answer these two questions:

1. Why is this value important to me?
2. How does this value show up in my life?

Are you done? Congratulations! You now have your first LL. Fold it up and put it away. Don't forget to let someone know there's a letter to be opened in case you "go" tomorrow.

What else can I put in my Legacy Letter?

Here's the great part: *There aren't any rules!* Every LL is as unique as the person writing it. And if, over the course of time, you're moved to add more of yourself to your LL, here are a few things to ponder:

- Beliefs
- Talents
- Skills
- Triumphs
- Failures
- What I'll miss
- Hopes for future generations
- Life's lessons
- I forgive you
- I ask for your forgiveness
- Love I want you to know

I know this can be tough. A wise woman friend said she might hesitate writing an LL because, "You're kind of admitting that you're going to, well, you know...*leave.*"

Dear Reader: I'm going to "leave." So are you. I know it. But, I don't plan on taking that trip for another 30 years or so. Just in case I get booked on an earlier flight, I want my LL done. I love the fact that it's in my drawer and my family and future family will get to enjoy it. I know they'll feel good confirming that some of that Robb spirit is in us too. What if I didn't write my LL? What if you don't write your LL? Our families may never have the chance to know us better, to laugh and cry with us. Don't take that away from them.

I climbed Mount Kilimanjaro in 2001. My tent mate was a new friend and a lovely guy named Don. Eight of us became very close and had a stunning time. Since then, each year we've traveled from around the country for a reunion over golf and adult beverages. On our thirteenth reunion, things were different. Don was in palliative care, loaded with prostate cancer.

During one of our visits, Don asked me about the idea of a Legacy Letter and said, "I really don't want to do it, you know."

"That's fine," I told him. I then recounted my story of finding my values, answering the two questions, adding a bit to my LL every six months or so, and feeling very happy that it was done, knowing my wife and family would have it a long time from now.

Don grew silent. Then he turned to me and said with the biggest smile I'd seen on him, "My first value is honesty." He began writing. I stayed silent for five minutes as he wrote, then left, never to see him again. He died two weeks later. I don't know if he ever completed his LL, but that enthusiastic smile stayed with me.

Okay, how do I create my LL and store it? For the sake of those who will enjoy your LL, there two methods:

The Envelope Please

Call me old-fashioned, but I bet that 500 years from now your descendants won't mind thumbing through those pages of paper that contain your LL. As such, write it with an ostrich quill pen, or type it into the electronic device of your choice. I typed my LL into my computer, printed it, put it in a sealed envelope addressed, "To be opened after Robb's been trampled by that herd of water buffalo," and put it in a drawer. As life moves on, I occasionally update my LL, but it's always in that drawer, the one my wife knows about.

Roll Camera 1

You might like your LL to be recorded on video, then stored on whatever digital domain is preferred; hard drive, SD card, USB stick, or on the 'Cloud'. Or, to ensure no one will ever see it, VHS or Betamax. You do take the risk of descendants 500 years from now remarking how weird you look, but *sticks and stones may...* well, you know.

Hire a video professional if you want to look glamorous, or use your computer's built-in camera, or a webcam. You can even use a smartphone. If you want a simple, yet workable video LL, without any expense, here's a solution:

RecordMeNow.org has an app that allows you to record a video LL on your computer, and structure it with themes and questions of your choosing. The app was quick to load for Mac and PC, and within a couple of minutes I was recording myself through my onboard video camera and microphone. The RecordMeNow app guides users through a variety of subjects, like values, reflections on relationships, messages of encouragement, memories, favorite moments, recipes, advice and of course, affirmations of love. You can write in your own questions, which, in the final video program, appear as graphics on the screen while you give your answer. It has the flexibility to let you create a very personal, rewarding and effective LL on video. RecordMeNow will then record your message to DVD and let you individually address copies to loved ones. And it's free.

The benefit I'll get out of my LL? Well, three things:

1. Knowledge – You will get to know yourself better. Your values, life experiences, strengths, struggles and achievements make you unique, and your family and those who follow will want to hear your story. Don't steal it from them.

2. Health – Several studies have found that talking about life experiences lowers blood pressure and strengthens the immune system. Telling your story can be cathartic… just one page!

3. Stories – You'll be remembered. There is satisfaction in a life well lived, and I believe that deep down we want our life to be remembered. The LL is a simple way to say, "I was here."

I know that without an LL my story will be long gone after I'm taken out by those water buffalo, an errant tidal wave or a simple little heart attack. The LL gives my wife, family and descendants an easy way to cuddle up with me again and be reminded of my values and life's story. We'll all smile.

When should I write my LL?

Um, do we have to go through this again? Remember the Legacy Clock, the speeding bus or the errant heart valve? Can I call you tomorrow to see if you're finished?

And, finally: If you knew tomorrow would be your last day on earth, would you like to leave behind a document telling who you were, what you learned, what your hopes for the future were, and who you loved? Would you feel better knowing that future generations would learn about you, and from you?

At the start of this chapter you might have wondered if you had a legacy to leave or a story to tell. Now, I hope you know you do. Those who walk the world after us will be hungry for our stories. As Pulitzer Prize-winning columnist Ellen Goodman wrote, "What the next generation will value is not what we owned, but the evidence of who we were and the tales of how we loved." You have built your own flame of knowledge. Let others light their candle with it.

Jason and Gretchen each wrote their LL some years ago, and kept them in a drawer in the home office. They asked their eldest daughter to write one on the eve of her marriage, and she did. The daughter gave a copy to her parents and it went into the drawer. Her new husband wrote one and a copy went into the drawer too. Their eldest son wrote his and it went into their new LL box on the home office bookshelf. Then the youngest son, at 18 years, completed his (and changes it every six months or so).

Jason and Gretchen's goal is to have everyone's LL in that box: children, grandchildren, even Gretchen's sister. They know that one day each of them will be read. "Our stories are in that box," said the youngest son, smiling.

So, if those buffalo get me, my eulogy is written. Just open up my LL and let me pour out.

And now that your story is written, what about all those other fascinating people in your life? They don't understand legacy stories like you do now, yet their stories should be found and kept, just like I did with Dad's book.

L et's move on to "Legacy 2: GATHER Their Stories" so they don't disappear.

Legacy 2: GATHER Their Stories

"My mother told me the other day that there's a lot she'd like to know, but there's nobody left to ask. The door to the past is closed."

– Garrison Keillor

Whose story do you NOT want to disappear?

You may remember that as we approached the year 2000 there was the Y2K scare? As the clock ticked from 11:59 pm on December 31, 1999 to 12:00 am January 1, 2000, the world was supposed to come to an end, sending us all back to the Mesozoic Era. It was thought that all computers on the planet would rebel at the entry to the New Millennium and would screech to a halt, along with every machine they ran, like planes, hydroelectric dams, factories, ATMs, street lights and the computer on your desk. I knew people who were preparing for Armageddon.

My wife and I spent that New Year's holiday with friends in a beautiful oceanside house on the Pacific Northwest Coast. If Y2K was going to bring down the Western world as we knew it, we wanted to be in a stunning environment with people we cared about. But as you'll remember, the clock struck midnight and the world went on. Those who had cached food and water in their basement had to bring it all back up and put it in their cupboards.

To get to know our friends better during that weekend, I drew up a series of questions that each would answer. They seemed simple enough, but as we learned, they had depth too. They were the catalysts for some tearful, and joyful conversations.

I asked them to tell us about:
- A movie that affected you;
- A book that affected you;
- A skill you will learn;
- An experience you will have;
- …and others.

The one question I remember the most was, "Tell us about a person who affected you?" My response to this was quick:

I met Dick when I was a journalist and broadcaster. He was about 45 years old when he walked into the station for the first time, and we urbanites looked at him with wonder and awe. His skin glowed. His graying hair, under a felt hat complete with grouse feather circular, was tied in a ponytail. He wore a buckskin jacket, wool shirt and pants, and a yellow silk bandana around his neck. His teeth were bright white, long before those teeth-whitening products littered the shelves. He smelled like the great outdoors; a mixture of pine, poplar and moss, and clean, warm air, like after a storm. He was well-educated, and read voraciously. Dick would become my outdoor mentor. For 30 years, off and on, I learned what to carry in my pack, what mushrooms were safe to eat, how to carry fire in the rain and how to survive if lost for days in a –20 degree frozen forest. It was good brain expansion for this urban lad. Dick taught me how to live in, and love always, the wild surroundings that keep me in touch with the earth. Dick affected me.

Then, Dick was gone, forever. Prostate cancer. Sadly, I, nor anyone else, had collected Dick's story – a story his children, grandchildren and all those who followed him could learn from. It would have been an amazing story of adventure, heroism, love and wisdom. Dick's story is gone, never to be gathered.

. . . .

Gather stories? Who, me?

Yes, you. But you needn't worry about having to morph into a journalist. In this chapter, you'll learn some simple skills to gather the stories you don't want to disappear. Those stories will inform, amaze and entertain people generations from now. They will learn about their forebears because of you. These stories will be your legacies too.

Okay, whose stories?

Have you ever thought, *I wish I'd asked them more about their life?* Or, *I'd love to know what it was like back then?* Unfortunately, most of us wake up to the idea of legacy story gathering too late.

Is there one person in your life whose story you don't want to disappear? Mom, Dad, an aunt or uncle? A great grand-uncle or a wild and crazy cousin? Patriarch or matriarch of the family? I'm not going to hold it to you, but who is the one person whose story you'd like to ensure doesn't disappear?

_____

This is the name of the person whose story I don't want to vanish.

Lost Story #1

These are my great-grandparents. They emigrated from Ireland around 1875, to the hard scrabble, swampy, mosquito-filled land of Northern Ontario, complete with muggy summers and bitterly cold winters. They had 13 kids, and five of them died before they were 15 years old. The other eight left when they could. Some moved to the Philadelphia area, and my grandfather, a strapping 18-year-old, to the West. That's all I know about them. No journals, no letters, nothing. My family would love to know about the life they led and the hardships they faced.

They'll say, "Why would anyone want my story?"

You may be asked this question. My answer would be, "Would you like to have known your grandparents', and your great, great-grandparents' stories? Would you like to know about their family, their schooling, work, home, holidays, joys and tragedies? Well, so will your descendants love to hear your stories." All of our lives and stories will be valued by those in the future because our lives are part of the reason they are where they are now.

> *"There was never yet an uninteresting life.*
> *Such a thing is an impossibility. Inside the dullest*
> *exterior, there is a drama, a comedy, and a tragedy."*
>
> – Mark Twain

Lost Story #2

They called her Hustler May. It seems that my grandmother was a very good golfer. In the 1920s and 30s, she'd climb the hill to the golf course with her bag of four irons and one wood, and then challenge the boys to a three-hole game. Three holes, best score, 10 cents. Apparently, she never lost. I say apparently because I don't have her full story, only slivers told by my father. Would her now great, great-grandchildren love her story? Yes. Would your great, great-grandchildren love the stories you gathered about those who were important to you? I think yes.

Technology now makes it easy to collect those stories so all can receive their benefits. Your storyteller will feel recognized and prideful that their story is "moving on." Generations in the future will feel connected, rooted and part of a larger picture. We can't just leave our future family looking at one picture and wondering, *What was it like back then?* We have a guaranteed audience who wants our stories.

"What the next generation will value most is not what we owned, but the evidence of who we were and the tales of how we loved. In the end, it's the family stories that are worth the storage."

— Ellen Goodman, Journalist

There are hundreds of studies that tell of the therapeutic benefits of gathering and telling life's stories. Narrative therapy was pioneered by psychologists Michael White and David Epston in the 1980s. It has shown to be healing for people to tell their stories because they gain a better understanding of their life's events. The benefit for you? The people you gather stories from will value their lives more.

In his book, *Like a Library Burning*, Scott Farnsworth affirms that, "We love those whose stories we know, and we feel connected to those who know our stories. The stories we help preserve and pass on will touch hearts, connect families, and change lives." The problem is that when they "go," that library disappears. That fortune in wisdom, experience, insight and life lessons is gone.

How do I gather stories?

Glad you asked. We'll follow the simple formula I've been using for 35 years. It's a formula that works. Follow it step-by-step and you won't feel overwhelmed. You'll actually enjoy it. You're going to draw out the stories that will have generations from now smile and say, "That was our Great, Great, Great-Uncle Herb." Whether you want to produce a one-page story after a one-hour conversation, a film that makes you the envy of Hollywood's A-team, a colorful book or a short and entertaining YouTube video, you can use this method to gather these stories.

There are three stages to produce that story, regardless of how you'll finally present it.

1. **Pre-production** – getting things ready
2. **Production** – gathering the story
3. **Post-production** – putting the story together

Let's go through these stages for the story you've decided to gather. You don't have to do any of this work. You may decide to hire a professional to gather and produce the story. We'll discuss that later in the chapter. But if you know a little bit about the process, you'll enjoy it more.

1. Pre-production – getting things ready

Pre-production means preparing to gather the story. Let's describe it with three elements: *Who, What and How:*

Who has the Story?

You've already identified the person whose story you want to gather. Let them know you'd like to have some conversations to collect some of their stories. If you sense reluctance, remind them of the joy and interest all would have if you could gather your ancestors' stories. You will promise to lead them gently down the path with some easy conversation and questions (we'll cover these questions in "2. Production – gathering the story").

Before production starts, the best research you can do is to browse their photo albums, along with photos that are hanging in their home. They'll usually represent high points in their life, so make note of them before you begin your conversations. And ask, "Is there anything you'd like me to look at before we begin?"

What Form can the Story Take?

Let's keep this simple. You're collecting the stories and then assembling them into a specific format. That format could be:
- A Legacy Letter (LL)
- A biography (chronological life story)
- A memoir (choosing a specific part of life, like military, career, family, dramatic event, etc.)

You could produce each of these as either written words on a page, an audio or video program. For instance, I produced a memoir of my father's war experiences. It became a "print memoir," a book. It could have been a video, but we decided on print as I hope people will read the book hundreds of years from now.

You could produce a video biography of your storyteller, highlighting their life with interview clips, photos, home movies, music and graphics.

Or, it could be an audio biography where we listen to them tell their story.

Or, it could be a print biography in a book form, including stories and photographs.

Print, Audio or Video?

One more thing: you could produce another format – an autobiography. This is your life story, containing much more content than an LL. An autobiography can also be done in print, audio or video. Right now, we're talking about gathering another person's story, but all that you learn here could be applied to gathering your own story.

How to Gather Stories?

You have some choices on how to gather the stories, so let's put them in perspective, take away any mystery and point out their benefits.

Joe Lambert is the founder of the Center for Digital Storytelling in Berkeley, California. One day, he found 18 boxes of material that told many stories of his parents' lives in the South during the 1930s.

"Now I can look online at everything that was in those boxes," he told me. It's an example of technology being a powerful tool for creativity and legacy-making. "We create the stories, and the stories will move into the future with technology."

You're going to sit down with your storyteller to gather their story. Don't worry about being a technical neophyte. Gathering the story is as simple as a good conversation. So, how do we gather that story?

Written Transcription

This method has you writing down, on paper, with a pen, all the words you hear from your storyteller. Or, typing it into a computer as you listen to the story. I don't recommend it. Sorry, too much work. This isn't the form of digital storytelling I was thinking of.

Audio Recording

Ah, the joy of the voice. With this method you record your storyteller's words. This is the most effective way to gather those stories. Those recorded words could become an audio memoir to be listened to by family hundreds of years in the future. Those words can be transcribed for use in an LL, a biography or any other printed form. Or, those taped words can become the soundtrack for a video of historical and contemporary images. Audio is so flexible!

Here's what you need to record your storyteller's voice:

- A digital voice recorder, a small, hand-held tape recorder that records a digital audio file.
- A lavalier microphone, which is hooked to the recorder. This is the small microphone that you pin on your storyteller.

You will find search terms at the back of this book, which you can use to find many suppliers for this inexpensive hardware.

After your interviews and stories are recorded in an audio file, you have some choices to make if you want to use those words in a printed piece.

- Transcribe – This means listening to and typing the words into your computer. If you have 2 to 25 hours of interviews, this could be quite tiring.

- Transcription services – You send the digital audio file to a service that will do the transcribing and typing for you. This could be expensive.

- Speech recognition – This is what I do, and it's magic. I record the storyteller, then put that digital audio file into speech recognition software. It immediately turns the audio file into text. Yes, editable words on the screen. I use Dragon NaturallySpeaking to do this.

Video Recording

I've produced video and film for over 30 years and know the final product can be memorable or terrible. In the future, your relatives will love seeing the real person; their face, voice and gestures. Your storyteller can really connect with their family of the future. Yes, you or a filmmaker in the family can shoot and produce the video. But if you're doubtful, I highly recommend hiring a professional who can ensure things go well the first time.

Here are a few things to think about in this pre-production phase:

- Lights! – Make sure your storyteller is well lit so we can see them clearly. Do a test on yourself and watch it on a TV. Do you look bright and alive?

- Camera! – There are so many options now, from shooting on your smartphone to a professional HD camera. Ensure your cameraman knows their gear. Again, pin a lavalier microphone on the storyteller and ensure it's hooked up directly to the camera. Do not rely on the microphone that's on the camera as it will be difficult to hear the storyteller.

- Action! – If you're interviewing the storyteller, do that only. Don't try to be host/interviewer/cameraperson/ audio guy/lighting guy, etc. Concentrate on gathering the stories. Let your technical crew (even if it's only one person) handle the rest.

So, to sum up pre-production:

1. Pick a storyteller:
Grandma, Grandpa, Aunt Mame or Uncle Joe

2. Pick a format:
Legacy Letter, biography or memoir

3. Pick a story-gathering method:
Writing, audio or video

4. Start gathering those stories!

If you're not comfortable recording and interviewing, StoryCorps may be the answer. StoryCorps is a non-profit whose mission is to provide people of all backgrounds the opportunity to record, preserve and share their stories. It works like this: You and your storyteller sit down in one of StoryCorps' booths in Atlanta, San Francisco or Chicago, or in one of their partner organizations (museums, libraries, etc.), or in one of their mobile booths that roam the country. Your 40-minute conversation is recorded on a CD, one copy given to you. One copy is preserved forever in the American Folklife Center at the Library of Congress where to date StoryCorps has archived over 50,000. StoryCorps also gathers the stories of those affected by serious illness in nursing homes, hospices, cancer centers, etc. as part of their legacy initiative.

2. Production – gathering the story

You now know whose story you want to gather, and the technology you'll use. In this second phase, you're essentially mining for diamonds, and you may be surprised at the gemstone stories you'll find. Everyone has a story to tell. There is healing power for the storyteller as they reflect and relive. There's joy knowing the memory and feelings will continue. *This is and was me. Pay attention. I want to share.*

You may decide to be the interviewer, or to hire a professional to gather the stories. Whatever your decision, read on, as the more you understand, the more you'll enjoy the process.

The one element that's necessary to gather great stories is a great conversation. You will lead that conversation with your questions; the stories will take you on a journey through your storyteller's life experiences. Hundreds of years from now one of your legacies will be that your future descendants are enjoying these stories.

Early in my career, I worked with two skilled broadcasters who knew how to draw out stories. One said of his interview technique, "I ask questions and then get out of the way!" Another said, "I'm in a canoe with a paddle, gently directing the way."

The best story gatherers know how to lead the way, and get out of the way. Here are four interview skills for collecting great stories:

Story Gathering Skill #1: "Tell me about..."

This is the only question you will ever have to ask. When you say, "Tell me about elementary school," or "Tell me about your siblings," or "Tell me about your first job," you are giving your storyteller the freedom to tell the story as they want to. That freedom will give their answer enthusiasm, energy and detail. You've gently guided them with one paddle stroke, "Tell me about…" and then got out of the way. For great stories, just use this question over and over. Here is a "Tell me about…" story:

I was doing the story of Charles' and Beverly's lives for their 50th wedding anniversary. I asked Beverly to tell me about when she first met Charlie.

"Well, we were on the pier at the lake, all of us kids, and then Charlie came on the pier and fell in, and we had to get him dry to go to a wedding…"

"Wait," I said. "Tell me about Charlie falling in!"

"Well," Beverly smiled, "we were all waiting to go to a wedding, and all the kids had gathered out on the pier in front of Charlie's cottage. It was a hot summer day. Charlie had a brand new blue suit on, I guess the first one he had ever worn. I can see it now. He wore a white shirt and a plain blue tie, and it was then that I really took notice of him.

He walked on the pier, I think I caught his eye, and he was fooling around with his friends and all of a sudden he fell in, or was pushed, or something. We all laughed and helped him out, and he was soaked. He had new black shoes on. His mother would be home in an hour to take us to the wedding, and she would be furious.

So Charlie ran in and got out of his water-logged suit and came out in his bathrobe. It was red. We hung the suit, his shirt, his socks, his underwear all on the line, hoping like heck it would all dry. There was a warm wind that day and in 45 minutes they were all dry.

Melisa, Charlie's big sister, pressed everything as we brought it in. She really loved him, and didn't want him to get into trouble. When his mom got back we all got in the car before Charlie's mom could really look at him, though he looked all right. His shoes weren't dry yet though, so he had to wear my brother's shoes, two sizes too big for him. But they were brown, not the black ones like his mother thought he'd be wearing! Charlie kept a good distance from his mother all day. I remember standing close to him at the wedding and I looked at him... I think I fell in love with him for the rest of my life."

All I had to say was, "Tell me about..." and out came the story. I followed up with, "Tell me about...":

- When you knew you were in love;
- Your first home;
- Your family.

"Tell me about..." will result in stories filled with enthusiasm, energy, pictures and detail. It is actually the only question you ever need to ask.

Story Gathering Skill #2: "Close your eyes and tell me..."

Sometimes your storyteller will have trouble remembering details. But when they "see" their stories again, they'll recall them much more clearly. For years I taught communication techniques using left-brain (logic and words), and right-brain (creativity and pictures) theories. We're all taught to speak with well-reasoned words. Closing our eyes allows us to see the movies of our lives. They're captured in our creative right brain so we can put them into words using our left brain.

If your storyteller says, "I can't remember," just ask them to close their eyes and tell you what they see. Ask them to describe the movie that plays in their head.

At gatherings of American and Canadian friends I've asked people if they would close their eyes to record their answer to the request: "Tell me about the first time you felt emotionally connected to your country's flag." The stories poured out about parades, quiet moments, sporting events, country fairs, 9/11, national birthdays and more. With their eyes closed, they described the weather, the people, the colors, the sounds and the events happening around them. And then, still with eyes closed, I asked them to sing the first few lines of their national anthem.

Oh, say can you see, by the dawn's early light...
By now the tears were flowing.
Oh Canada, our home and native land...

All were happy and fulfilled to tell their story. They were almost joyful at watching and describing the movie in their mind. Closed eyes = pictures = a movie = story.

So, try the closed-eyes technique when you're gathering from your storyteller.

"Close your eyes and tell me about...":
- Your father and the tractor;
- The day you bought the car;
- That Paris experience.

Story Gathering Skill #3: Facts, Memories and Meaning

Each story can be filled with facts, memories and meaning. Facts are the simple details. Memories are the people, places and events. Meaning is the significance, and why it mattered. Your legacy stories will be rich if you get all three. Let's look at an example from Beverly's and Charles' summer's day experience:

Facts: Charlie fell in the lake, got dried off, and had to wear oversized brown shoes.

Memories: Beverly's story does a good job of telling her memories and details of the event.

Meaning: Beverly might have said the meaning of the event was her finding out that Charlie was kind, good humored and resourceful. And, that stuck with her until he finally asked her out six years later.

Most of the stories you receive will be made up of facts. At this stage, you want to ask the questions to get the memories and the meaning. For example:

Facts: Dad brought over some friends and they built a barn.

Memories: "Tell me about your memories of this barn raising." Use the closed-eyes technique if you need to.

Meaning: "Tell me about what this meant to you… the good friends and new barn."

Here's another example story from my own experience.

Facts: Three days after 9/11 eight of us went to Africa and climbed Mount Kilimanjaro to raise money for a charity.

Memories: Some of our group had lost friends in the twin towers tragedy. We were on the first plane out of our city on September 14. On the mountain, the weather was hot during the day, cool at night. The food was so-so. One of the group was quite sick on day three, but recovered. On day five we reached the summit at sunrise and had a minute's silence for those who lost their lives. We were sad, and exhilarated. We hit one golf ball each and they flew forever. It was a long hike down from 19,340 feet to 9,000 feet for our last night on the mountain.

Meaning: Our friends lost their lives during the 9/11 disaster, but we wanted to salute them by pushing through something hard. We looked to the sky from the mountaintop and said, "Goodbye. We will try to make the world a better place."

. . . .

Story Gathering Skill #4: W5+H

As you saw at the beginning of this book, a guaranteed way to gather a tale from your storyteller is to say, "Tell me about":

- WHO was in this story;
- WHAT happened;
- WHERE it happened;
- WHEN it happened;
- WHY it happened this way;
- HOW it affected you and others.

Legacy Research Walks

The more you know about your storyteller, the better you can draw out the stories they really want to tell. As a result, you'll both enjoy the process of setting those stories free. When your legacy stories are heard, read or watched hundreds of years from now, your family of the future will love the details, pictures and emotions those stories bring. Here are a couple of research techniques I call "walks" to get your storyteller in the mood. Each of these walks can be audiotaped or videotaped, or just make notes about the items, so you can ask about them later on tape.

Walk #1: Photo Album Amble

Almost everyone has pictures of their life, from beautiful, clear, digital images, to fading shots of the past. Your opportunity is to collect the stories of those pictures before they fade too. Those pictures will elicit stories of joy and sorrow, big events and small, friends and foes.

Each one of those images has facts, memories and meaning. Here's what I'd say:

- "Tell me about that lady in this picture."
- "Tell me about your memories of Aunt Helen."
- "Tell me about the meaning Aunt Helen give to your life."

Reviewing pictures with your storyteller can provide a richness you never imagined. It will connect both of you to the past, just as these stories will connect your future relatives to you.

Walk #2: Heirloom Ramble

My parent's home was filled with art and mementos they had collected during 65 years of marriage. Every one of those treasures had a story. After I completed Dad's book, my niece spent hours walking through the house with Dad as he told the story of each piece – where it came from, the memories of receiving it and what each piece meant to him. These pieces conjured up many new movies in Dad's mind, and sometimes a fair bit of emotion. I call this an "heirloom ramble."

The benefit of an heirloom ramble? With both our parents gone, each piece that was distributed to me and my four sisters has a story to it. As we pass these down to our children and theirs, the stories will go with them.

Your Story-Gathering Conversation

And now the fun part – gathering and listening to the stories with the skills we just described. You can hire a professional to help gather the stories, and in some cases that may be the best thing to do. I'll tell you how to find one later, however, you now have the skills to gather some fascinating, memorable and legacy-building stories. These are the skills:

- "Tell me about…"
- "Close your eyes and tell me…"
- Facts, memories and meaning
- W5+H
- Photo album amble
- Heirloom ramble

You have learned what I learned in my early journalism career: questions are a storyteller's best friend. Good questions send a storyteller off and running with enthusiasm. Now, let's look at questions for three different scenarios:

1. One-sitting memoir
2. One-sitting life story
3. Multiple-sitting life story

One-Sitting Memoir

A memoir, according to my *Webster's Dictionary*, is "An account of something noteworthy." This is basically one chapter of your storyteller's life story. It could be an inspirational tale, a story of a lesson learned, an observation of an event or just plain bragging about an accomplishment. My dad's book was a memoir about his war experience.

You can sit down many times with your storyteller, but let's assume you'll only have one fruitful conversation and want to know the whole story when you're done. As you now know, the best way to ensure you get the whole story is to collect the W5+H with our favorite question:

"Tell me about":
- WHO was in this story;
- WHAT happened;
- WHERE it happened;
- WHEN it happened;
- WHY it happened this way;
- HOW it affected you and others.

As you listen to each section, know that you can flesh out the story by saying:

- "Oh, tell me about that."
- "I've got the facts of the story. Tell me about your memories of it. What did this mean to you?"
- "Close your eyes and describe it."

One-Sitting Life Story

You might only get one two- to three-hour conversation with a family member or friend. If you want a wide view of their life, here are some broad statements that will let them tell their story.

"Tell me about":
- The world you grew up in;
- Your parents;
- Your siblings;
- Your schooling;
- Your first job;
- Your career;
- What you were really good at;
- The happiest time in your life;
- The toughest time in your life;
- The most significant person in your life;
- Your greatest accomplishment;

- What you'd change in your life;
- What you're thankful for;
- What you'd say to a relative 100 years from now.

These look simple, but you can go deeper by delving into each one of them.

Show them these topics and let your storyteller pick the first one to discuss. They'll choose the one they're most enthusiastic about, the one they have more memory of. That will get their storytelling juices flowing.

During any answer there will be many opportunities to say, "Oh, tell me about that." Remember Beverly and Charles? Keep your other techniques in your back pocket to help give more detail to the stories.

Multiple-Sitting Life Story

This scenario allows you to sit down with your storyteller a number of times to gather the full story of their life. Usually, the easiest way for them to remember the story is chronologically, from childhood to present day. You will find that after your first conversation their memory will get better and their stories more detailed. There are thousands of questions you could ask, but these will get the storytelling engine going.

Childhood (0–13 years)

"Tell me about your":
- Home;
- Family (parents, siblings);
- Grandparents, uncles, aunts;
- Pets;
- School;

- Friends;
- Celebrations (holidays, birthdays);
- Summer holidays;
- You as a child;
- Your fears/joys.

In the free download of *The Legacy Starter*, described at the back of this book, you'll find questions for other ages:
Adolescent (13–19 years)
Early adult (20–39 years)
Middle adult (40–59 years)
Senior (60–80+ years)

So, you now know who the storyteller is, and know how you'll gather the story (write, audio or video). As the story gatherer, you can simply sit back, listen and be amazed.

There Are No Stories Without Listeners

This is a talking stick, a sacred tool used by Native Americans and First Nations people. Whoever holds the talking stick has the floor. All others must be silent and listen. So it is for you, the story gatherer. As your storyteller speaks, be silent. Often the best question is silence.

Depending on their age, your storyteller will be processing the facts of their stories, and the pictures will be flooding into view. Give them time to hear their silence, and they will eventually fill it with new facts and pictures. If you feel it's time to break the silence, the best thing you could say is, "Tell me about what you've been thinking." Or, "Tell me about the pictures you've been seeing in your head."

3. Post-production – putting the story together

Post-production means putting the story together in a form that will last so it can be enjoyed now and far into the future. Your choices are to post-produce the stories you gathered into a final print, audio or video format. Each one has its own benefits and costs. Some you can do yourself and for some you may choose to hire a professional. The key is you've gathered the stories. Now, let's make them easy to pass along.

> *"For the first time in my life I felt that my past would have importance and value for my future grandkids. This gives meaning to my life; those stories are of value."*
>
> – JS, client of Rebecca Robinson, personal historian, Guelph, Ontario

Analog to Digital

In the last three generations, our methods of communications have evolved from telegraph to telephone, desktop to laptop, fax to Facebook and teletype to Twitter, but most importantly, from analog to digital. In analog terms, print was glue and artwork. Audio was comparable to magnetic tape recorders; video too, from 2" to 1" to 3/4"; then Beta and VHS. Each analog method was expensive, as you usually needed a professional who understood the pitfalls. I was one of those professionals. I made a living helping clients pre-produce, produce and post-produce their content. It was a frustrating minefield if you didn't know your way through it.

That's all over. Now, everything is digital. Not to get too complicated, but digital is just 1s and 0s. Every word, picture and sound is expressed as a string of 1s and 0s, or a binary form. When I typed these words they went on the screen in a digital format. All we need to know is that digital storytelling makes it easier to post-produce our stories into formats we can give to the world; formats that will sound and look great when viewed by our family hundreds of years from now. So, let's look at three methods of post-producing your legacy stories (audio, video, print), and how you'll distribute them.

Audio

Situation: You have recorded your storyteller and have one, or several, digital audio files of the interviews you collected. The next step is to transfer digital audio files from your recording device to your computer. Need help? Ask a 14-year-old.

Audio Production

After listening, there may be sections of audio you just don't need, like stories told twice. These sections can be edited from your files with an audio editing software package. There are free and inexpensive software solutions on the Internet that you can download. Search terms at the back of this book.

Audio Distribution

So, you now have some great life stories, as told by that jolly raconteur and everybody's favorite, Uncle Jack. How do you get these stories to family and friends? Easy. Burn the audio file to a compact disc (CD), just like the ones your favorite music comes on. However, that's only feasible if you're burning just five CDs. If you're burning 500 you'll find many companies that will get them done very cheaply. They can also put the audio on a USB stick, another way for your family to transfer it to their own computer. Or you can just email or upload the file to Dropbox or Google Drive for all who want to place it in their iTunes folder or make their own CD.

"Grandma was a fabulous cook, and at 86, still very active in the kitchen. In six afternoons, over a period of six months, we recorded the making of 44 of her favorite recipes, complete with laughter and lots of tasting. Her voice was rich and playful. She died at 89, and for Christmas I gave everyone a *Grandma's in the Kitchen* CD. Everyone cooks along with them, listening to Grandma's voice. I still cry when we make her favorite, bouillabaisse."

– PB, Calgary, Alberta

. . . .

Video

Situation: You have video footage of your storyteller. You need to get the footage into your computer for editing, and if you've gone this far, you probably know how to do this. If not, there's always that 14-year-old, or you could find a professional to help.

Video Production

I love editing. If you collected some great videotape from an enthusiastic storyteller, it's as much a joy to watch now, as it will be for your family tomorrow, and a couple of hundred years from now. In its simplest terms, editing is just lopping out the parts you don't want (repetition, stumbling, stories not well told, etc.). Editing also involves adding – adding music, graphics, computer animation, scanned pictures, old film and other video footage, then producing your master, the final show. This video could be six minutes or 60 minutes. I have four words of advice: Keep It Simple + Shorter (K.I.S.S.). Longer is not necessarily better.

Video Distribution

It's digital, remember, so your family a zillion years from now will be able to watch your video. As with audio, you can place the video on devices, such as DVD, to view on your TV, and USB sticks to transfer the video to a computer and view on its screen or the TV. You could upload the video to a website or family blog for anyone to see, wherever they are. You can up-load the video to the 'Cloud' for family members to download to their computers – your 14-year-old executive producer can help here. While you've got them working for you, have them upload the video to any number of video-sharing websites (YouTube, Vimeo, etc.).

"This DVD ensures our future generations will know my grandfather as a real person. I felt more connected to relatives I never knew. They're alive to me because of his memories."

– FH, client of Steve Trainor, personal historian, Rock Island, IL

Print

Situation: You have text of your storyteller's words that came from your conversations. You transcribed the stories yourself, had someone do it or used speech recognition software. You might also have great pictures that come with the stories. Now you want to put them all together in a format everyone can enjoy.

Print Production

As described in "Audio" and "Video," the first thing to do is edit the material, as the spoken story can be a little unwieldy when it's transcribed into print. Stories may be too long; your storyteller may ramble.

Home and Online Publishing

With editing complete, you can have the stories formatted and printed on regular paper, and ideally you know how to scan some of the pictures and import them into the file too. You can print it at home or print and bind it at an office supply or stationery store. With a little bit more patience and skill, you can produce fabulous-looking books (legacy books, birthdays, anniversaries, etc.) by uploading pictures to one of the many publishing systems available online. These systems are easy to learn and you can cost-efficiently produce a small number of very attractive books.

Professional Publishing

With this option, you hand your material over to an editor, designer and printer. This is the method we used for my father's book. I did the interviews and edited the material.

I then gave the material to a publisher (who happened to be my sister), and she coordinated the design and printing of the book. If you hire a personal historian to help with the gathering of the stories, they will have their own publishing methods, including design, printing, binding, etc.

"I've known my grandmother for all of my 42 years. I learned so much about her and it opened up hours of conversation between us. The family will really be amazed and happy we took the time to have this book done professionally. It will be treasured forever."

– CS, client of Sarah Merrill, personal historian, Providence, RI

• •

Phew! I know this chapter on gathering has been a lot to absorb. Whose story to gather? What technology to use? How to draw out those stories? But, it's really not that difficult once you've decided on the person whose story you want to hear, and then start gathering it with an illuminating conversation.

So, let's move on to the largest category, "Legacy 3: CREATE New Stories". This chapter will show you how to create a wide variety of legacies that truly fit you. These legacies don't start with story, but they end with story. That is, you can create stuff that salutes your values, skills and talents, and also fits our definition of legacy:

Your legacies will connect you to people, will enhance your life and theirs… and will continue to positively affect lives when you're gone. Yes, your legacies and you will be remembered.

Once created, each one of your legacies will begin to tell its own story. We know that stone turns into sand and blows away. Wood rots and decomposes into the earth. However, something as fragile as the story of each of your unique legacies will go on and on.

Legacy 3: CREATE New Stories

*"I want to leave a legacy. I just don't know what!
Tell me what I can do. Give me some examples!"*

I've heard this many times. I believe it's a yearning to craft a more meaningful life, a life full of legacies that will live throughout time; legacies you can be proud of because they reflect you, benefit others and make you happy.

There are many stories of people around the world doing fabulous things, changing the lives of thousands for the better. I have no doubt you can do that too. But legacies we hear about in the media seem so big. You may think, *too big to do on my own.*

So, where do you start? You may have your Legacy Letter already started, or completed. You may be gathering the memorable story of a family member or friend. Now, with this third method of legacy-building, it's time to use a formula that makes creating your new legacies, and their stories, easy.

Remember the formula for happiness: those who are connected to other people and are fully using their skills and talents are the happiest among us. So perhaps a conscious effort to use our skills and talents with others is the way to build our legacies? We can inspire others with our excellence, while creating and sharing a deeper connection.

Legacy-Building with Talents and Skills

In "Your Raw Materials – Values, Skills, Talents" in Chapter 2, you identified some of your talents and skills. Here are mine:

Robb's talents:
1. Gardening
2. Writing
3. Outdoor Enthusiast

Robb's skills:
1. Media Production
2. Marketing
3. Public Speaking

Write yours down again to remind yourself of what they are:

My talents:

1. _____ 2. _____ 3. _____

My skills:

1. _____ 2. _____ 3. _____

You can create legacies of any size by using your skills and talents. This becomes deeply personal; it becomes part of who you are. And that makes it so much easier. When you clarify your distinctive set of skills and talents, you prove that you are completely unique. You are in the legacy-creation zone. Anything is possible.

So, how do we start creating our legacies with our skills and talents? *With a talent or skill that I have, what legacy can I create that connects me to people, benefits all of us and makes me happy?* I suggest following a linear, flexible and doable formula:

Talent/Skill **legacy**

The key is beginning small.

The Garden

One of my talents is gardening. At the entrance to our street is a big, ugly cement guard and a six-foot metal fence to prevent you from driving into a forest and over a cliff. We thought it would be nice to cover this with flowering plants, but upon calling the municipality, were told, "No budget."

So I went to the local gardening store and told them about our plan. We were willing to buy the vines and plants, but they said "No, we'd like to donate them." I then went to the corner with shovel and fertilizer and started to plant. Within minutes there were about a dozen neighbors there with shovels and trowels, all saying, "It's about time!" and "This was so ugly," and "What can I do?" In half an hour, it was done.

I appointed a VP of Watering, VP of Mowing and a VP of Garbage Collection from among the neighbors. We've just finished our third year. We now have new connections among ourselves and, perhaps more importantly, a new story to tell. When we drive by, we smile. And, if the water buffalo get me tomorrow, the flowers of Legacy Corner (as we now call it), will rise every year, positively affecting others when I'm gone. A simple legacy? Yup.

This little legacy reminds me of a quote by my favorite quotation guy, Mark Twain:

"Don't part with your illusions. When they're gone, you may still exist, but you have ceased to live."

I looked for personal legacy stories for this book, big and small, and found them with individuals and members of a variety of organizations around North America. They range from small neighborhood legacies to international charities. Each legacy creates a story; one that connects the legacy builder to others, adds joy to their lives and puts a smile on their faces. Each legacy and its story will live on to enhance future lives. As you read these, keep your skills and talents in mind, for each story might be a catalyst for your legacy-building imagination.

George Sanders has played trumpet for about 40 years in bands, philharmonics and at the odd football game. His wife noted his collection of six horns and made a suggestion: "Why not teach someone so they'll take them away?" George liked the idea and so he began talking up "a free trumpet course" around the neighborhood. In a month, he had five students in the garage, ages 16 to 72, beginning eight Saturdays of music education and horn playing. As of this writing, he had completed seven sessions. "I love it," he says. "They love it too."

Talent/Skill: Playing the Trumpet
Legacy: Introducing music into the lives of those who might never have learned an instrument. Four students are in orchestras or symphonies. Big band music is heard more and more around

their small community. There's a waiting list to join the Saturday sessions. George's friend, Rick, will take over if the water buffalo get George.

John Cardie called his 14-year-old grandson and his friends to the table and said he would buy them each a sports car if they could complete one challenge. They agreed.

"First, each of you crack an egg into a bowl," he instructed them, "then scramble it." After they were done, he said, "Now, I'll buy each of you a car if you unscramble the egg."

They looked bewildered. "We can't Grandpa."

"That's what it's like trying to reverse a bad decision," John replied. He then taught them, through winning at the game of checkers, the value of smart decision-making, and how good decisions would help them in life too.

Talent/Skill: Playing Checkers
Legacy: John's book, *How to Beat Granddad at Checkers*, helps adults teach kids thinking and planning. "Once you make a move, you can't take it back," *says* John. Kids learn to recognize a "dumb move from a smart move, and how to plan their next move so it counts, in checkers and in life."

Don Foster knew that the rec center and swimming pool in his small prairie town of 3,200 were falling apart. There was no money to make improvements. He gazed across the fields at the potato processing facility; a big employer in town. He went to them with an idea. The company donated 40 acres of land and a bunch of seed potatoes. Don helped form a committee of farmers to cultivate, fertilize, harvest, grade and sort the spuds, then sell them back to the potato company. That year, 102 people showed up on harvest day to sort the potatoes, and they made about $40,000. The next year, $83,000, and on it went. Don formed the community foundation, and last we talked they had an endowment of $1.8 million, donating hundreds of thousands of dollars to local charities.

Talent/Skill: Financial Planning
Legacy: A community foundation ensuring healthy kids in an active community.

Ken Burch was well-known as an expert cribbage player. One day, while visiting his aunt in a care home, he was challenged to a game by 92-year-old Peter. Soon, a handful of residents were behind Peter, cheering him on. It was an energetic, boisterous, joyful afternoon. Ken was hooked. Now, once a month on a Saturday afternoon, Ken and his 16-year-old son, Kevin, return to the home for the Saturday Crib-Off where eight residents play them. There's plenty of laughter (and the odd argument by the very competitive players). On crib days it becomes a care home like no other.

Talent/Skill: Playing Crib
Legacy: A tournament that generates joy, laughter and connection. Ken and Kevin agreed to replace themselves when they leave so the tourney goes on, and on, and on.

Shannen O'Brian worked for non-governmental organizations in Africa and recognized that inefficiency and corruption were two major problems. She wanted to help the people of Ghana with two critical needs: clean water for their health, and education to take girls out of the cycle of poverty and injustice. She founded createchange.ca, and was highly innovative in how she raised funds. Now, thousands of girls have graduated from school, water is flowing and people are healthier in mind and body. Shannen's goal is to convince funders, with passion and facts, that extreme poverty will be pushed aside with strong, intelligent, hard-working, happy and healthy people.

Talent/Skill: Determination and Curiosity
Legacy: Educated and healthy girls are creating changed families, changed villages and a changed country.

Glenn Walker opened several very old boxes that belonged to his family just before they were to go to the dump. Inside, he found papers, photographs, deeds, census records and more, dating back to the nineteenth century. It was a puzzle to be solved, so the hunt began to fill the branches of the family tree. That tree is now healthy and growing after Glenn discovered and contacted almost 400 new members of the family.
Talent/Skill: Amateur Genealo-

gist
Legacy: A larger family connected to the past, to each other, and to future members.

Vivian Finlay was a child living in Burma (now Myanmar). Her grandfather, Luther Hodges, promised her a trip to the U.S. if she would write a travel report, just like he had taught her mother to do years earlier. She had already read many of Grandpa's travel reports about every country he visited while president of Rotary International. Vivian wrote her first report, and was hooked. Vivian's husband, their seven grown children, 22 grandchildren, two great-grandchildren and numerous nephews and nieces were hooked too. Many of the family travel stories have been collected into books with the knowledge that future family members will value the thoughts, feelings and observations that were written many years ago.

Talent/Skill: Travel Writing
Legacy: Vivian's grandfather's legacy is an enthusiastic, connected family now, and an informed family in the future.

Allison Thomson is a structural engineer. Her brother's 14-year-old son was in a car accident, or rather, a skateboard and car accident, while he and his friends were competing on a local paved street. There was no skateboard park in the city. Allison did some research, drew up the plans, found space in a park with the city's permission, and did some crowdsourcing to raise the money. The following spring, the mayor cut the ribbon on the "coolest park ever!" About 300 boarders were off the streets, using the park till 9 pm when the lights blink, signaling, "Time to walk home."

Talent/Skill: Engineering
Legacy: Allison's legacy is generations of safer skateboarders, some of whom have moved on to national competitions. Plus, Allison's career changed direction when she became a sought-after designer of outdoor public spaces.

Aaron Wong was visiting his sister in a town about 50 miles from his home. They went for a walk in the local bog. As a biologist, Aaron was amazed at the variety of birdlife, counting about 40 species that day. But, no one else knew about the richness of the population. That night, they hatched a plan. Aaron would provide all the biological data for each species, and they'd approach the local community foundation to fund signage and wooden walkways. The foundation located a sponsor (another legacy builder) and a year later The Bog Walk welcomed thousands of visitors.

Talent/Skill: Biologist
Legacy: Enriched knowledge for every visitor who learns about the importance of protecting the environment for the bog's 175 bird species, 41 mammals, 11 amphibians, 6 reptiles and approximately 4,000 invertebrates.

Harpinder Dhaliwal had seen the pictures on TV a hundred times, of families and small children displaced by war or disaster, sometimes freezing, but always without warm clothing. Harpinder knitted six full suits for children aged two to four years and mailed them to a disaster relief organization. The letter of thanks she got back convinced her there was a huge need. She encouraged a dozen friends to knit clothes one Saturday a month. The clothes that travel to the unfortunate families have two words sewn in them, "With Love."

Talent/Skill: Knitting
Legacy: Warmer children who will grow up healthier. A dozen knitters looking for new opportunities to spread their love.

Add a Value

Now, let's go one step deeper. You read earlier that the happiest among us are those who are connected to others, who use their skills and talents, and live in tune with their values. Rick Hansen (story coming up) is building his legacy to cure spinal cord injuries.

"If I want to leave a legacy, what should I do?" he asks. "Make sure my values and actions are in sync."

Creating a legacy in tune with one of our values lights a fire deep down; it brightens our lives because it brightens other's lives now, and in the future.

It's simple really. Just follow this formula:
Value ➡ Talent/Skill ➡ Legacy

"How wonderful that no one need wait a single moment to improve the world."

– Anne Frank

My wife and I were holidaying in Cambodia. While driving back from Angkor Wat, I looked at the parched land and asked our guide what people did for water. He told us that this was a big problem, that surface water was dirty and caused much disease. He spoke of a local man who was beginning to drill wells in the small villages, but didn't know his name. In half a day we'd found the man; my wife and I are pretty good researchers. His name was Pahl, and he took us out to see a couple of the wells he'd drilled. One of my values is opportunity. I like to help create them for myself and others. It was immediately obvious that fresh, clean water from a new well created opportunities for the dozen or so families who used the water to stay healthy and create new income. For example, the clean water allowed them to create new products with their sugar cane, which means products for tourists like us. We gave the small amount of money he needed to drill a new well and were delighted to see the result in a picture he sent a few months later.

Value: Opportunity
Talent/Skill: Research
Legacy: Healthier people with a brighter future.

Chris Greicius was seven years old in 1980, and dying of leukemia. Chris told his mother, Linda, that his one wish was to be a policeman for a day. Well, word got out to some Arizona Public Safety Officers and U.S. customs agents, and soon Chris had a made-to-measure officer's uniform for his helicopter and patrol car rides. He then received his motorcycle officer wings by riding his battery-powered mini-motorcycle through the cones. Shortly after Chris' funeral, Linda and four others were inspired to form the Make-A-Wish Foundation where, at the time of printing this book, over 350,000 wishes have been granted in the U.S., Canada, and around the world. I spoke to the founders who agreed on the value that drove them, and what their main skill was (of the many they used).

Value: Giving Back
Skill/Talent: Credible spokesman, passionately telling the story
Legacy: One small act of giving back has resulted in hundreds of thousands of children, families and friends around the world, experiencing the hope, strength and joy that comes from a child's wish. And of course this legacy continues on.

Larry W was the husband of a long-time friend. I didn't know him well because we lived a great distance apart, but still went to his funeral. I was surprised to join about 300 people at the service, as he'd been a quiet, unassuming man. But then the speakers began, and we heard over and over, "I would not be alive if it wasn't for Larry." Larry was an addictions counselor, and a very good one. He never gave up on people. "He listened as no one ever has," they said. He guided his clients to a feeling of self-worth so they could take pride in their life once again. The people at this service were sober because of Larry. Many of them became counselors because they wanted to do for others what Larry did for them.

Value: Contribution
Skill/Talent: Listening
Legacy: Healthy people who continue to help others

Kathy Morris loves cooking. She wanted to pass on her knowledge so the poor and disadvantaged, who know only processed foods, could enjoy nutritious, inexpensive meals. Once a month, she borrows a kitchen from a community center and asks several organizations to send up to 10 less fortunate moms and dads who would like to learn about, prepare and eat a delicious dinner. With food donated by three stores, the class prepares and eats their meal, amidst much laughter. They receive a grocery bag full of ingredients and recipes to make the meal again at home. All parents leave with good food ideas, more knowledge of nutrition and its long-term value. This has grown to six community centers, and Kathy enjoys coordinating her growing legacy.

Value: Health
Skill/Talent:
Cooking and
Coordination
Legacy: Informed
and healthier
families.

Dr. Jack Hutchinson is my dentist. He closes his office once a year and takes his staff to perform dental work on the poor, at his expense. In the last few years, Jack and his staff have performed dentistry for over 10,000 people in Guatemala, Nicaragua, the Philippines, Uganda and Mexico. "We focus on 10 to 14-year-old girls," says Jack. "We give their smile back. By changing their appearance, we change their self-esteem." Not to mention their health for the rest of their lives. "We fill cavities, pull teeth, teach how to floss and brush. The payback is when they turn around and give you a big hug." Part of your legacy, Jack? "Yes," he said. "I've run into other dentists, doctors and private companies who say their lives have been affected because of what we've done.
What could be better than that?"

Value: Giving Back
Skill/Talent: Dentistry
Legacy: Improved self-esteem,
health and personal growth
for those who might never have
experienced it.

John Wood was trekking in Nepal in 1998, when he visited a school of 45 students, which had a library with no books. The headmaster said, "Perhaps one day you'll come back with books." And that was all it took. John left his employer and took with him all his professional attributes: thinking big, goal setting, how to run a lean operation with a big effect. John founded roomtoread.org, a non-profit organization that has, at the time of writing this, impacted the lives of more than four million children by establishing nearly 9,200 libraries, publishing 433 original local language children's titles in 21 different languages, representing the distribution of more than 4.1 million books and building almost 1,200 schools. The organization is now one of the fastest-growing, most effective, and award-winning non-profits of the last decade. "I was just an ordinary guy with a dream," he said. "Create your legacy while you're alive, when you can see it and enjoy it." Lesson from John: one of your legacies could appear on your next walk, so keep your eyes open!

Value: Education and Fairness
Skill/Talent: Asking for support (and collecting good people)
Legacy: Using literacy to lift people out of poverty, into health and democracy.

Robert Genn was an internationally known artist specializing in paintings of the West Coast and Rocky Mountains. He was also a passionate communicator who loved connecting and sharing. In 1998, he sent a letter on creativity to five people and it spread like wildfire. Soon, Robert was sending out two letters a week to 50,000 subscribers. He wrote on the physical, spiritual and emotional side of being an artist, with the simple goal of nurturing and empowering creative people, as well as the rest of us. The letters were irreverent and playful. "The whole thing is a joy," said Robert. New subscribers of the twice-weekly letters would read,

"Absolutely free, no strings. You'll get the valuable twice-weekly letter and be joining the world's most active arts community." Before he died in 2014, Robert had sent over 2,000 letters. Artists in every state of the U.S., every province of Canada and in at least 115 countries have visited www.painterskeys.com to sign up for the letters. As a perfect example of his legacy carrying on, the letters continue twice a week. Robert's daughter, Sara, an artist in New York City, writes one letter a week and uses one from his collection.

Value: Connecting
Skill/Talent: Communicator
"With joy, play and courage," said Robert.
Legacy: To explore our creative selves, and to reach.

Lemons = Legacy Lemonade?

Now, back to that happiness thing. What about when life deals you a bunch of lemons? Is there some legacy lemonade to be made? Can we create legacies out of circumstances that have hurt us deeply? When we're down and life has kicked us, can looking for and creating a legacy help us get up?

"The happiest people I know are dedicated to dealing with the most difficult problems," says Rosabeth M. Kanter, a Professor at Harvard Business School. "Turning around inner city schools. Finding solutions to homelessness or unsafe drinking water. They face the worst of the world with a conviction that they can do something about it and serve others." Those are special kinds of legacy builders.

"They are inspired to tackle impossible challenges because they care about the outcome," says Kanter, "and happiness comes from the feeling they are making a difference."

So, can we build a legacy when life throws us a challenge that should probably bend or break us? Here are three stories of legacies created to meet difficult challenges. These stories are all from my backyard. You'll have stories like these around you too.

Rick Hansen was in a car accident at 15 years of age, which paralysed him from the waist down. When he came to terms with his new life, he set new goals for himself. From 1985 to 1987, Rick rolled his wheelchair 25,000 miles (40,000 kilometers), through 34 countries during the Man In Motion World Tour to prove the potential of people with disabilities. His 26-month journey inspired hundreds of thousands to make a difference. He then formed the Rick Hansen Foundation (www.rickhansen.com) and has since invested over $300 million toward spinal cord research, accessibility projects and quality of life initiatives. "My legacy?" says Rick. "A world where people with disabilities enjoy health and live in an accessible and inclusive society."

Value: Making a Difference
Skill/Talent: Communicator
Legacy: An accessible and inclusive world

Len Gross was diagnosed with prostate cancer in May 1992. He wanted to talk to other men who had experienced the disease, but couldn't find them.

"You hear you have cancer, and everything's a blur." After surgery he said, "We have to get men talking. This is a silent killer." Len discovered an informal group that needed some leadership, so he became the chair of the first support group in his home city of Vancouver B.C. A few years later, he founded the local

Prostate Cancer Foundation (www.prostatecancerbc.ca) and was its longest serving director. Support groups started to mushroom and Len became a founding member of the Prostate Cancer Network of support groups who help thousands of men each year get the information they need to make informed choices. Len is a walking encyclopedia of treatment options and leaves every man more knowledgable, calmer and hopeful about the future.

Value: Helpfulness
Talent/Skill: Listening
Legacy: Three organizations that help thousands of men each year cope with prostate cancer.

Kerry and **Ginny Dennehy** lost their 17-year-old son to suicide on March 2, 2001, after his short battle with depression. "Kelty was a normal kid, therefore it can happen to anyone," said Ginny. Teen suicide is at an alarming high, but once depression is recognized, 80% can be successfully helped. Kelty's parents are devoted to sharing their experiences with others, and the mission of the Kelty Patrick Dennehy Foundation (www.thekeltyfoundation.org) is the prevention of depression-related suicide in young people. The Foundation has raised and spent millions of dollars toward care, treatment, education and research. It's helping those who suffer, and others to better understand. "We are the foot soldiers of depression," says Ginny.

The Kelty Patrick Dennehy Foundation

Value: Making a Difference
Skill/Talent: Speaking Out (repetitively, passionately)
Legacy: Depression is treated as a disease and lives are saved.

I know all of these legacy builders personally. I stand in awe of what they've done, and how their legacies continue to grow.

In the section "Raw Materials," you were asked to identify your values, skills, talents. I also asked colleagues on my email list to identify theirs. About 75% of the list let me know what their values, skills and talents were. I then asked them to dream of a legacy they could create with one value and one skill or talent. Here are a few:

Name	Value	Talent/Skill	Legacy
Bruce	Growth	Soccer Coach	Bring in two World Cup coaches annually to help local team
Allan	Caring	Organizer	Gather neighborhood empty bottles for street people
Anna	Freedom	Educator	Money management mornings for low-income single moms
Chris	Creativity	Designer	Right-brain design sessions for community planners and the public
Peter	Conservation	Handyman	Fix all issues for 10 local non-profits
Chuck	Contribution	Team Builder	Develop a community substance abuse prevention strategy
George	Enthusiasm	Cooking	Recipe and tip book for senior's home volunteers
Leah	Compassion	Organizer	Begin football program where there is none

Name	Value	Talent/Skill	Legacy
Walt	Encouragement	Teaching	Takes at-risk youth into healthy family
Georgia	Freedom	Connecting	Fund three African doctors' training in North America
Eddie	Achievement	Guiding	Six youth learn responsibility while mountain climbing

Now, let's dream a bit.

Before you read ahead, imagine a legacy you could create. You know your values, skills and talents. Combine them and let your imagination wander. What could be a crazy, impossible, fun and wonderful legacy that would connect you to people, and benefit all?

Here are a few imagined legacies I could create with my personal "raw materials" lists:

My Value	My Talent/Skill	My Legacy
Adventure	Writing	Set up a scholarship for North Pole global warming and environmental reporting
Wisdom	Outdoor Enthusiast	Once a month, an evening Kid's Walk in the Woods to learn what's "out there"
Health	Gardening	Monthly Salad Tuesdays in the neighborhood; a learn-about-these-healthy-veggie recipes get-together, and meals that we all share

What imaginative legacy would put a smile on your face? No, you don't have to create it, just imagine it!

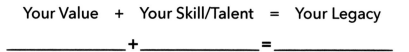

At this stage of our journey together, I hope your dormant forces are fully awake. I hope the mystery of legacy has given way to the clarity of a thousand possibilities. Whether TELLING your Story, GATHERING their Stories, or CREATING new Stories, you now have the tools to salute your values, and show your unique skills and talents to the world.

> "When you are inspired by some great purpose, some extraordinary project, all your thoughts break their bonds: your mind transcends limitations, your consciousness expands in every direction, and you find yourself in a new great and wonderful world. Dormant forces, faculties and talents become alive, and you discover yourself to be a greater person by far than you ever dreamed yourself to be."
>
> – Patanjali, Indian philosopher

The hardest part is SEX!

Ah, that got your attention. One quick question: Do you think males and females look at this legacy thing differently? Let's find out.

LEGACY AND SEX
The Male and Female Approach

*"We are all human beings and in this sense equal.
We are not, however, the same."*

– Dr. Christopher Ounsted, English physician

M ale and female – the same? I've been married 29 years, and would vote no. The question of this chapter is, *Do men and women look at legacy differently?* Is one sex more likely to build stories, and one sex more likely to build stuff?

You'll remember that ethical wills were written to reflect blessings, moral directives, even burial instructions. Later, they grew to include the writer's values, personal and historical information. Women weren't allowed to write a legal will until recent times, and so these wills were eventually authored by women in the form of letters and books written as gifts for their children. Women became the ones who passed down the family stories.

Rachael Freed told me both sexes are interested in telling stories, but said women "...yearn personally and communally for connection across time and space. We yearn to know our personal history and to know ourselves as part of history. We yearn to know that our lives have significance now, and to understand our spiritual connection and purpose."

Today you'll find the majority of personal historians are women; specialists who will work with you to produce your story, or that of Grandma, Grandpa or Aunt Matilda. Not all, but most.

I think men are a bit more cautious about story, though I have worked with some of the best male story builders and storytellers in the world. We just need to think about it for a while as our natural instincts tell us there are other legacies to build. But, when men craft personal stories – stories we don't want to lose – men are caught in story's gentle leghold and want to share as much as women.

My colleague, Roy Prevost, teaches leadership, but one day he gathered a group of men for a session called, Your Father's Story. The participants were meant to write factual stories, but it instead became very emotional as they each told, and wrote, of their father's shortcomings and long comings – the good, bad and ugly. It turned out to be an illuminating and cathartic experience as they had negated the legacies of their fathers – the effect their fathers had, not only on them, but also on their siblings, their family and their lives.

The stories that surfaced were aha! stories, as in, "Now I understand him better," or "That's why he was the way he was." Grasping the issues they had with their fathers seemed to illuminate their own lives, and might give some light for generations to follow.

John Gray said in *Men Are from Mars, Women Are from Venus*, "A man's sense of self is defined through his ability to achieve results. A woman's sense of self is defined through her feelings and the quality of her relationships."

Generally, it seems that women have been the more natural connectors and collectors of story, looking back to preserve and create a family legacy. Men, on the other hand, seem to look forward to creating a personal legacy. Story gathering and telling has been the woman's strength in legacy, and stuff was the man's strength. But, are women moving from storytelling to stuff, and men from stuff to storytelling?

My father was always concerned about where his and Mom's stuff would go when they died. We did elaborate lists on who would get what. After we completed Dad's book, his story, his focus changed. Instead of stuff, he realized every piece in the house – every painting, every piece of jade, every photo in an album – had a story. Instead of leaving stuff behind, he wanted to leave stories behind. We just never had enough time to get to all those stories.

Statistics say women generally outlive their mates by five to seven years, and this has changed the face of philanthropy as women now generally control the purse strings of their estates as well. For instance, more family foundations are headed by women now than at any other time. And they want those estates to produce legacies that are meaningful, while they're alive. Men still gravitate toward stuff when thinking legacy and contribution, but I think collecting and ensuring their stories are told is becoming a much stronger urge.

I fear generalizing, but I think there's an awakening happening. We all come from different cultures, careers and life experience. We bring to legacy different values, morals and focus, whether we come from a traditional, blended or same-sex family. The roles are changing, the lines are blurring and the needs are being modified. Legacies will always be part story and part stuff. But more importantly, legacy stories will help us get to those *aha!* moments. Whether you TELL, GATHER or CREATE those stories, they'll serve to connect you with others. It doesn't really matter if male or female.

So, who needs to be involved in building a legacy story? Let's review:

TELL Your Story – It's you. No one can do it better.

GATHER Their Stories – The gatherer is the person who has that key quality – curiosity. Ask your family, "Who wants to gather Grandma's story?" The person with their hand up knows curiosity will ensure those stories will be enjoyed hundreds of years from now.

CREATE New Stories – It's you again, male or female, but with others too. With your legacy in mind, ask others, "Will you join me?" That's connection. And it will become their legacy too.

In the next three chapters, you'll learn about organizations that will help you build your legacies, and how to use your resources to get the job done. You don't have to be rich, but know this: you have the ability to be as honored a philanthropist as those you read about. Let's find out how.

LEGACY AND MONEY
Everyone's a Philanthropist

"To give away money is an easy matter and in any man's power. But to decide to whom to give it, and how large, and when, and for what purpose and how, is neither in every man's power nor an easy matter."

– Aristotle

Remember the old idea, the more money or stuff you leave behind, the bigger your legacy? Many philanthropists leave sizable estates to good causes, enhancing the lives of those who follow. But, the big difference here is timing. When we just leave our resources (money, real estate, securities, etc.) behind, we won't be there to enjoy their effect. Know this: your legacies can be created using your resources, and enjoyed by you right now.

In the next three sections, let's talk about money by describing:

- The one who's going to spend it – you, the philanthropist
- The organizations who will help you spend it on your new legacies – your dance partners
- The smart way to spend it – the giving tools

We've learned to create legacies using our values, skills and talents. Now let's add our resources. If you have more resources than you need, maybe now's the time to use them to build legacies that will put a smile on your face and many other's faces, now, and in the future.

Value ➡ **Talent/Skill** ➡ **Resources** ➡ **legacy**

By adding resources to our formula, it doesn't mean you have to be a rich philanthropist. Small amounts can have a big impact.

What's Philanthropy?

The word philanthropy comes from the Greek *philanthropia*, which means, "Love for our fellow humans." The English Oxford Dictionary defines it as, "The desire to help others, especially through donations of money to good causes."

Philanthropists have the ability to make a difference in people's lives because of their money and other resources. When they add these to their values, skills and talents, it's a powerful legacy-building formula.

You may have written a check to your favorite charity and hoped that your donation will help the cause. Philanthropy is a more planned and strategic approach with a long-term perspective. It's about money, yes, but you set goals with rational and thoughtful decision-making. It's important to know your long-term vision and the legacy story you want told as a result.

I could be a philanthropist?

Short answer, yes. To be an effective philanthropist, you will know how to use your resources to build legacies that will connect you to others, strengthen your community and make a difference for all those who follow. You don't have to be in the same league as Bill Gates or Warren Buffett to use philanthropy to build your legacy stories. But it's important to know what your legacy-building resources can do, whatever the size.

As you know, there's a powerful advantage when you're clear on your values, skills and talents. Philanthropy is about what's in your heart, not just about what's in your bank account. It simply makes legacy creation more joyful.

In a moment, we'll learn how "a money guy" uses life's stories as a way to clarify values so people can use their resources to create legacies.

If I'm a philanthropist, don't I need to know a lot about money?

Have you ever sat down with a financial advisor and felt, well, a little stupid? It's a complicated industry with terms that may cause your eyes to glaze over, leaving you nodding and telling your advisor, "Whatever you feel is best." That advisor may want to see your assets grow, but may know very little about you, or how you'd like to affect the world with your legacy-building. And, as an important aside, your advisor can still be paid, year after year, even if your legacy's portfolio value is shrinking and your legacy goals are in jeopardy.

In North America there are over 570,000 registered investment advisers and brokers, up to 300,000 general financial advisors offering fee-based financial planning, over 38,000 certified financial planners and over 80,000 specialized insurance advisors.

When your discussions are only focused on transactions and money, it can leave you deeply unfulfilled and disenchanted with legacy and philanthropy. Your deeper needs haven't been talked about. Scott Farnsworth of Sunbridge Legacy, a finance guy who really knows story, says there's often a client service gap between you, the legacy-building philanthropist and your financial advisor.

"Money isn't the most important part of a client's wealth," says Farnsworth. "The elephant in the room is their humanity, the richness of their lives, the depth of their concerns, their values, vision, wisdom and purpose. All these run deeply through their lives."

> "To put the world in order, we must first put the nation in order; to put the nation in order, we must put the family in order; to put the family in order, we must cultivate our personal life; and to cultivate our personal life, we must first set our hearts right."
>
> – Confucius

So, we need to know what those deeper concerns contain. If we're going to use our resources in legacy-building, our advisors need to know too. *The Allianz American Legacies Study* notes that our increasingly disjointed and hurried pace of life has sparked a deep yearning, especially in Boomers, to act on issues of significance. We need to connect head and heart. Then our legacy-building will be more meaningful.

Understanding Our Personal Stories

> "A man is always a teller of tales, he lives surrounded by his stories and the stories of others. He sees everything that happens to him through them, and he tries to live his own life as if he were telling a story."
>
> – Jean-Paul Sartre

As you know, your legacies will last far into the future because their stories will continue to be told. Using your financial resources to build legacies doesn't change that. But in this case, we really need to know what makes us come alive. And to learn that, it's good to examine the stories of a variety of areas of our life. Those stories will help us understand ourselves; they'll help clarify our deepest values and uncover life's purpose and passion.

And now, there are financial advisors who understand this. Stories drawn from our experiences are a gold mine of understanding for the attentive financial advisor.

Becoming Human Beings

The *Allianz American Legacies Study* noted that stories of our life lessons, wisdom, values, morals, etc. are 10 times more valuable to Boomers than financial wealth. So, it's a big advantage for a financial expert to tap into what's important for their clients. When we clearly paint the picture of the legacies we want to leave, the financial tools are there to build them. This is what Farnsworth insists on with his clients.

"I help lawyers and financial planners become human beings," he says. "Story was pounded out of us in finance and law. Now they're learning the power of story, and the value of sharing stories." Farnsworth has created a learning series called *Priceless Conversations* where a financial advisor presents you, the perhaps-not-yet-clear legacy builder, with questions that inspire deeper conversation. This series features brief, but meaningful, conversations about what's on your mind and in your heart. They allow the client to share stories, wisdom and experience in areas like:

- The meaning of money
- The meaning of wisdom
- The meaning of success
- My values
- Our family values
- Children
- Childhood years
- Adult children
- Grandchildren
- Love
- My faith or spirituality
- My alma mater
- Sharing
- Giving
- Pets
- Our plan
- Turning points
- Treasures
- Tributes
- Wishes
- Veterans
- Year in review
- My business
- Celebration
- Angels and heroes

Two Examples of Priceless Conversations:

Turning Points

This is a conversation about the hinges of our lives, those experiences that sent you in new directions. It's a look back at the significant moments and how they shaped you as a person. What beliefs did you incorporate into your life because of these changes? Values now become clearer: adventure, learning, giving back, challenge, spirituality, etc. One of my Turning Points was standing in the middle of the Australian desert for two days trying to hitch a ride. The daytime flies were relentless. The evening mosquitos unremitting. I began to write in my pad; thoughts became prose, ideas became poems. I learned to know what I was thinking by writing what I was thinking. The seeds were planted. I would become a communicator (of some sort). And some of my legacies will definitely be in the promotion of literacy.

Angels and Heroes

Each priceless conversation is a short, story-based conversation about the most important issues on your mind and in your heart. Anne tells the story of herself as a rebellious 15-year-old who left home, intending on hitchhiking across the country. She was picked up by a middle-aged man who, upon hearing her story, talked of the danger, violence and change-of-life that could happen so quickly to her. He drove her home. Years later, because of this priceless conversation, she confirmed her values included safety, love and connection. Her legacy focus was now clearer: the underprivileged, street kids, safety in the community.

"It's simple," says Farnsworth. "If a financial advisor understands your stories and can connect the dots to the appropriate financial advice, legacy-building will be much more fulfilling and effective."

"Many people are in an uninspired giving rut," said Jason Franklin of boldergiving.org. "When people don't know what's important to them, or don't know the values that lead their lives, they're seldom excited about their giving. The result can be giving as a routine, writing a small check where they're not engaged in their giving, and certainly have no plan to create some personal legacies," says Franklin. The solution? "Spend time to learn what's important to you. Create legacies you'll feel connected to."

So, that's the first part of building legacies with your resources; being very clear on your needs. Now, what if you know you'll need help building one of your legacies? How do you find the right legacy-building partner? Who do you dance with? Will that be a charity or a foundation?

Your New Dance Partners!

"Give generously, but not indiscriminately.
Select carefully those worthy to receive your gifts."

– Lucius Seneca, Roman Philosopher, 4 BC – 65AD

We've talked about creating your own personal legacies, like the story of your grandparents, your corner garden, a small charity to help the disadvantaged, or trumpet practice in the garage that helps someone become a philharmonic star. These are your personal "I thought of it" and "I did it" legacies.

But instead of doing it on your own, you can also work with an established charity or foundation. They have the cause, organization and experience. They can be local, national or international. Working with a larger organization can help you build legacies that change lives by enhancing the environment, the arts, education, health, sports, the disadvantaged and much more.

Charities and foundations aren't just places where you write a check and walk away. You can do that, but let's shift our paradigm a bit. You may know your values and want to create a legacy in line with them, but don't know what to create. Charities and foundations can help you find it. If you already know the legacy you want to create, they can be there to help you get it done. They can help you connect your values and passion with a legacy you believe in. They can be great dance partners.

So, who are they?

Charities

In 2016 there were about 1,740,000 non-profit organizations in the United States and Canada. About 1,040,000 are registered public charities working in areas like arts and culture, education, environment, faith, health, human and social services, international development, sports and recreation. Other non-profits are made up of private and public foundations, chambers of commerce, civic leagues, etc.

Each year we give billions of dollars to non-profits so they can do their work. You've probably had the experience of writing a check and hoping it will do some good. In a few pages, you'll learn a much more effective method.

Our goal here is to assess how you can work with a charity to create a legacy you'll be proud of; one that's in tune with your values, will connect you to others and will enhance lives now and after you say, "goodbye."

So, what charity? Well, as I sometimes say to my wife who wants something done now, "Hang tough." Let's take a look at another option: foundations.

Foundations

Foundations have been around since the time of Aristotle, but it's only since the twentieth century that they've begun to address the real problems in our society. Foundations are non-profit organizations who make grants to unrelated organizations, institutions or individuals for scientific, educational, cultural, religious or other charitable purposes. Generally, a foundation doesn't get involved directly with a charitable activity, but gives grants so charities can carry out their work.

"A foundation is a body of money completely surrounded by people who want some," says Dwight Macdonald, United States writer and author of *The Ford Foundation.*

In general, there are two types of foundations: private and public.

Private foundations are managed by their own (usually) unpaid trustees and directors, and are generally funded (endowed) by one source, like a family or corporation. They help other non-profit organizations reach their goals. Two examples are family and corporate foundations.

A family foundation is defined by the Council on Foundations as one whose funds come from one or several members of a single family, and whose focus is the philanthropic goals of its board. Family members who serve as trustees or directors receive no compensation.

A corporate foundation receives funds from its parent company, although they are legally separate entities. Generally, its giving usually reflects company interests. For instance, its programs often benefit the employees, families or communities where the company is doing business.

A public foundation receives funding from a variety of sources (hence, public). It's managed by a board of directors and staff, and is a grant-making public charity, making grants to other unrelated non-profit organizations.

There are many types of field-specific public foundations that serve specific populations. Perhaps you've written a check to your local hospital foundation to help it build a new wing or acquire some badly needed equipment. Many public foundations are often attached to hospitals or universities.

Community Foundation

I think the biggest opportunity to experience the benefits of creating a legacy, of any size, is to work with a public community foundation. Just consider, *Is there something in my community I would like to see created or improved? What would help some, or all, enjoy our community more because of what I can do?*

A community foundation grows by donations of separate donors, and its focus is the long-term benefit of the residents in the town or city you live in. With a community foundation you can establish your own endowed fund (like a mini family foundation inside the community foundation) to help you become a more strategic, long-term legacy builder. You can take advantage of the foundation's administration (staff, reports, accounting, etc.) while you use your funds to improve the community.

In 2016 there were almost 900 community foundations in North America (United States +/– 700; Canada +/– 180). They are tax-exempt public charities whose focus is to identify current and long-term needs in their community, then work to create the future they want. These foundations gather long-term endowment funds from individuals, families, businesses and organizations. They grant funds to a wide range of organizations to create and maintain vital elements of their community.

Community foundations are all about quality of life. They bring people and talents together to stimulate new ideas in the arts, recreation, health care, education, safe neighborhoods and a healthy environment. They want to see your community legacy come true, now, and a hundred years from now.

The search term to find the foundation in your city is *(your city's name) community foundation.*

There may be some legacy stories on the foundation's website. Do they get your imagination going? I ran across a hundred stories. Here are a couple:

Eva Simmons received a large inheritance when her uncle died. Eva liked her life and had no plan to stop working in children's aid as a counselor, negotiator and networker. She was always interested in making life better for underprivileged children, and set up an endowed fund with the local community foundation. Eva works with the foundation to fund organizations that provide music, education, recreation, summer camps and theater for at-risk kids. Eva's been doing this for 20 years.

Value: Making a Difference
Skill/Talent: Understanding the difficulties of children at risk; an advocate with public relations skills.
Legacy: Many children's lives enhanced.

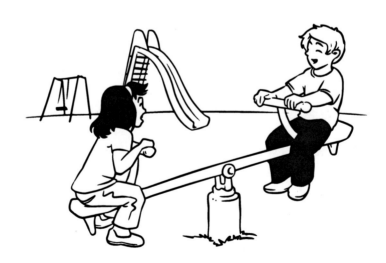

Ralph Roberts was up on the stage New Year's Eve with 25 fiddlers, all from his extended family, when he had an idea. Ralph was a middle-aged electrician, and knew very few electricians and plumbers were being trained to take the places of those retiring. He told a humorous story of a world without plumbers and electricians, and then talked all 25 family fiddlers into donating their normal Christmas spending to an endowed fund in their family name at the local community foundation. The fund chips in for apprenticeships and awards scholarships as an incentive for students to enter the trades. The fund is healthy and growing with the family's Christmas-giving program.

Value: Commitment
Skill/Talent: Storyteller
Legacy: A healthy trades population and 25 family members living, "We can do it" lives.

Their Cause. Your Legacy.

You know the normal method of helping a charity or a foundation: write them a check, walk out the door and hope they will effectively use the money to further their mission.

There is another way. Build one of your legacies with them. Your legacy will be something that furthers the mission of your chosen charity or foundation. It helps them accomplish what they're meant to do, but couldn't do without you.

"The key is finding something you're passionate about," said Scott Harrison of charitywater.org. "Poverty, local housing,

education, health, children. Find an issue where
of service and go deep. Make a lasting impact wit
talent and resources."

So, you've clarified your values, skills and talents. You know
of a charity whose work you appreciate because their mission
fits with your values and needs. You have a project you'd like
to see completed in partnership with a community foundation, or would like to take on a project they suggest fits with
you. You are energized and passionate to have an effect, and
know that connection, happiness and better lives will be your
legacy. You have a legacy project in mind and are wondering
what your next step will be.

Join me on a journey that may change your life. Head over to
the charity or community foundation you've chosen and ask
their executive director or chief executive officer one of these
three questions:

1. Skills/Talents: "I have these skills and talents. Is there a project
    you want done that I can make happen with these skills and
    talents?" One foundation's chief executive officer told me
    that these people are known as *knowledge philanthropists*.

2. Your Project: "Do you need a project done that I can make
    happen with my resources?"

3. My Project: "I have an idea for a project that I think fits
    with your mandate. And, I have the resources to make it
    happen. Are you interested?"

"A charity loves to hear a donor say, 'How can I help you accomplish your mission?'" says David King, chair of givinginstitute.org. "It's important to listen to what the organization needs. Sometimes the donor's needs don't fit with the organization's needs."

One thing to keep in mind is, "Donors can also put a charity or foundation through the hoops," said Bradford Smith of foundationcenter.org. "Your specific gift could cover costs for maintenance, administration, etc. There may be no income for that new overhead, and it needs to be supported too."

> *"Don't ask what the world needs; ask what makes you come alive, and then go and do that. Because what the world needs are more people who have come alive."*
>
> – Harold Whitman

Let's assume you really believe in a charity's mission, but don't have a specific idea in mind or certainly don't want to cause more overhead with your legacy gift. If you ask, "What do you most need?", you might be surprised by the answer. It could be a new MRI machine or, "We need to hire a fundraiser." Your legacy of a very healthy charity or foundation in the future might begin with, "Okay, I'll pay the salary."

"Go find something no one else wants to pay for," advises Scott Harrison, "like overhead. Your legacy will promote a healthier, more effective organization."

Whatever question you ask, and whatever answer you get, the legacy you build will open doors to new people, ideas and opportunities. Oh, and remember that legacy = happiness thing? Probably some of that too.

Picking Partners

There are two halves in this equation: you and them.

Partner 1: You

Before you ask one of the previous three questions to a non-profit chief executive officer, before you open your checkbook or volunteer your time and talent, go back to the values we covered in "Raw Materials" (page 65). Are these values still you? Do they still ring true?

Ask these questions again:

1. Why is this value important to me?
2. How have I lived it?

When you know your values and why they're important to you, you'll know when you find an organization that shares those values. Your gut will tell you it's a good fit. I came across this myself in a most unexpected way.

When we founded the Make-A-Wish Foundation in Canada, it was just shortly after the first wish had been granted in the United States. I began doing wishes, but really didn't understand why I wanted to do wishes. It just felt good. It hit me hard one night when I recognized the value deep inside me that I was saluting.

A seven-year-old boy with cancer wanted to see a famous singing group, so I arranged tickets, hotel, limousine and a nice dinner for the family. He brought his parents and twin brother. During intermission I took the family backstage to meet the group and soon the tiny baldheaded boy was singing up a storm with them. He knew every song. His twin brother joined them and his parents and I sat back and watched the smiles and happiness they hadn't seen for two years. All they'd seen, and all the little boy had experienced, was pain and tests, and intravenous tubes. When I put them in the limo at the end of the evening, they were electric. The family had never had so much fun.

I went back to my car, got in and cried like a baby. The work I had put in was nothing compared to the joy that was created. Clearly, one of my strongest values was joy. I loved creating joy, and wishes were the way to do it. We got a call about three months later. The little boy had died. I was sad for the family, but happy for them too. They would remember that joyful evening for the rest of their lives.

Smart legacy builders identify their values, and then become quite specific about the change they want to affect, on their own or with a charity or foundation. For example, I'd like to see cancer eliminated. Who wouldn't? But I know I can't accomplish that on my own. My legacy needs to be more specific, more doable. I'm a prostate cancer survivor. One of my values is wisdom. So, at the time of writing this book I'm helping some prostate organizations tell their story better so men are informed about the benefit of being checked by at least age 50. It's smart to be tested early. I hope my small legacy will be healthy men telling other men, telling other men, telling other men, and so on.

Once you know your values, then ask yourself a simple question: "What is important to me?" The environment? Education? Underprivileged kids? Our vets? The elderly? The hungry? Animal welfare? Literacy? Your neighborhood? Special-needs children? Emergency aid? Sports? Music? Youth leadership? Single mothers? Clean water?

Now, combine a value with a cause that's important to you. I learned by pure luck to tie my value of joy with sick kids. Another value of mine is wisdom. Along with my personal experience, it's been rewarding to use my cancer wisdom to affect men who want to stay healthy.

Consider where you want to build your legacy. In your neighborhood? In your country? Internationally?

Let's recap the steps:

1. Connect your value with a cause you have a passion for.
2. Connect with an organization whose mission supports that cause.
3. Connect with a project that both you and the organization are excited about.

You're on the way to some fulfilling legacy-making!

Partner 2: Them

If you want to work with a charity or foundation, they could be just around the corner. You may have worked with or donated to them before. However, if you don't have a partner to work with and want to find one, remember that all charities are not created equal. Some walk the talk better than others.

The Internet is a great tool for learning about and choosing a charity. The challenge is dealing with the copious amount of information. Here are a few sites to help out:

www.charitynavigator.org
www.guidestar.org
www.bbb.org/us/charity
www.givewell.org
www.greatnonprofits.org
www.myphilanthropedia.org
www.charityintelligence.ca
www.smartgiving.ca
www.charitycan.ca
www.canadahelps.org

Each of these sites has a different method of rating a charity, including their accountability, clarity of communications, effective use of their resources and finally, their impact. Some sites go deep and some go wide; deep in detail and wide in the number of charities they rate. Others just incorporate donors' comments on a specific charity, resulting in a popularity vote, which can be dangerous if you want to learn about a charity's real effect. Other sites you'll find are simply a cash register; you can donate to your favorite charity through their site, and they take a few dollars for helping you do that.

It's unfortunate, but many givers generally know very little about their charity when they decide to write a check. *But we're legacy builders, not just check writers.* Your decision on who to build a legacy with shouldn't just come from the heart. Yes, we'll get there, but let's find out a few things about the charity or foundation you're considering so you find a winner, the best-in-class.

Does the organization you're considering:

- Define its mission and programs clearly?
- Have measurable, clear goals and challenges?
- Have a strong board with broad experience that is actively overseeing a clear strategy to meet their goals?
- Detail their current finances, revenues and expenses?
- Clearly describe the meaningful change it's making in people's lives? If they can't convince you of this, it might be frustrating for you to begin legacy-building with them.

"The challenge for the legacy builder is to find high-performance charities," says Ken Berger of Charity Navigator. "You want to work with a charity that will engage you, and get you to a level of involvement that you've agreed upon. For the legacy builder, it takes some diligence and research to find the right fit."

Charity Navigator is America's largest charity rater and has built a rating system called CN 3.0, based on financial health, accountability and results. Berger told me "Charity Navigator uses this rating system to help legacy builders make wise decisions in choosing the charities that are most worthy of their donations."

Then there's the old saw (cost of administration or overhead). In an open letter at overheadmyth.com, several organizations say that when we focus solely or predominantly on overhead, we starve charities of the freedom they need to help the people and communities they're trying to serve. Is a non-profit who spends 13% on administration doing a better job than one spending 18%? We can't say that. As a legacy builder, we need to focus on the charity's transparency, governance, leadership and most importantly, results.

Now, to find that organization. This is where the hunt gets fun.

You know your values and want to find an organization that shares them. A variety of the sites listed earlier categorize non-profits as most-followed charities, charities expanding in a hurry, charities worth watching and highly rated charities with low-paid chief executive officers, etc. It can be very interesting to surf through websites of hundreds of charities. You can also search for charities working in the area you're interested in, such as animal rights, literacy, music, education for the underprivileged, medical research, children's rights, etc.

When you've found the non-profit you like, are satisfied with their answers, and ideally have spoken with them in person or on the phone, now's the time to:

- Go with your heart
- Trust your gut

This is the organization that will help you build one of your legacies. Your legacy project fits with their mission. They have the same values as you. Your skills and talents may be used. You can see your legacy in the future and you like it!

And now what? Well, a story, of course.

My wife and I fell in love and got married. We've led a pretty lucky, adventurous life. However, we have disagreements. And, I know exactly why that happens. We're not taking the time to ensure that we understand each other and our needs. It will be the same with your new legacy partner, that non-profit you've spent the time researching to ensure the fit is just right. You're getting "married" to create a new legacy. So, continue talking and asking questions to make sure you're building the legacy you envisioned. By the way, my wife Kim and I are still talking, 28 years later. We continue to build our legacies, just like you.

So, you've clarified your values, skills and talents. You've decided to TELL, GATHER or CREATE your next legacy. You're going to either do it on your own, or you're going to work with a charity or foundation.

And now you're wondering about, yup, money! Can you still be happy, *and* tax smart? Let's look at some smart giving tools.

The Giving Tools

*"We make a living by what we get.
But we make a life by what we give."*

– Winston Churchill

Remember we noted that the concept of legacy seems to have been taken over by the financial industry? Their focus: how are we going to package up all your money and other assets in your will so they can be left behind when you "go"? Presuming that legacy is just money is the old version of legacy, instead of *leaving* a legacy, you now know you can *live* a legacy.

I'll make three assumptions:

1. You know you can find happiness, connection and fulfillment when you TELL Your Story, GATHER Their Stories or CREATE New Stories with your values, skills and talents.
2. Because you're reading this book, you're probably at a stage in life when you have resources, such as savings, stocks, bonds, artwork, real estate, etc.
3. If you had a choice between a) paying taxes on the growth of those resources, or b) using that growth (money) to create the legacies you want to create, you'd probably choose b).

Opportunity Lost

Mary was a widow in her early 90s, a tireless volunteer at a homeless shelter for women and children. She arrived twice a week, like clockwork, to do whatever needed to be done. The kids didn't have a playground, so Mary made it her business to raise the necessary $40,000 for the equipment. She organized dozens of church bake sales and raffles but, sadly, died before reaching her goal. When her will was read, all were surprised that she had left the shelter $100,000. Mary didn't think she could afford to pay for the playground herself, but she could have. If she had worked with a financial planner who knew what was important to her, Mary could have donated the money while she was alive and even saved on her taxes. She could have swung on those swings with the kids. She could have enjoyed her playground legacy, and then left it to affect generations to come.

A key point here: Mary could have been 35, 45, 55 or 65. She could be any age. Creating legacies now means you can enjoy them long before you "nod off."

"All of us can be more adventurous, strategic, and involved in our legacy creation," said Jason Franklin of Bolder Giving. "When you learn how to give, you inspire others with the joy of giving."

Our job is to clarify the legacies we want to build, define the resources we'll use and find the help we need to be a smart legacy builder. It just takes a little planning.

Planned Giving

The terms planned giving and gift planning refer to the planning necessary to give a gift to a charity or non-profit that provides advantages for you and capability for them. Planned giving helps meet your philanthropic goals, and balances personal, family and tax considerations.

You can plan to give gifts while you're alive, but about 85% of planned giving happens with estate planning and in wills, after you're gone! Everyone should have a will, and you should have legal and financial planning advice to ensure that what you want to happen when you "go"

"Money is like muck – not good unless it be spread."

– Francis Bacon

does happen! A well-planned will can eliminate taxes and guarantee that the charities or foundations get the gifts you leave them.

But we're not here to talk about wills. You are a very much alive legacy builder. You want to create legacies, enjoy them and way down the line, leave them to affect other lives.

In my legacy seminars, this is where I had to be careful not to let eyes cloud over. Money was a cold and private affair. Planning to tax-efficiently take advantage of your assets, or use them for legacy-building, was the domain of the pros. A gift-planning pro is a great asset to have in your hip pocket, and having a little bit of knowledge is just as important. So, stick with me.

You're pumped about some legacies you'd like to create that are in line with your values. You may have to tap into your skills and talents to see them happen. Some of those legacies you'll create on your own, with your neighbors or with a charity or foundation. Some will need resources – like good old money. So, what are the smart money tools you can use to build your legacies?

"It can be daunting," David King of The Giving Institute told me, "but there are many ways to find the dollars to build legacies now that could last forever."

I'm not a money guy, nor is this book a financial how-to. I will describe a few ways to use your resources for legacy-building, but the list of money tools is by no means complete. You'll need to find an independent planned-giving specialist, or one at the charity or foundation you choose. Or, maybe your own well-versed accountant knows the tax implications of each one of these tools.

The key question you should ask yourself is, *How can I tax-efficiently use some of my resources to make this happen?*

The Situation

You've decided on the legacy you'd like to build. It's in tune with your values, it's going to cost money, and you want to build a legacy tax efficiently. Your legacy might be:

- New playground equipment in a local park.
- A school in an underdeveloped country.
- A machine needed in your local hospital.
- Scholarships for smart, underprivileged kids heading to college.
- An annual fund to keep a symphony orchestra going.
- Ongoing support for a Safe Streets program.
- A new softball field and yearly funding for the girls' team.
- An adult literacy class.
- Sponsorship of the annual Christmas parade.

You may need to work with a foundation or a local, national or international charity to get it done.

The focus of this book is legacies you can enjoy now. So, to get them done now, and tax efficiently, let's use some Smile Now tools. For those legacies that you arrange to be created after you "go," we'll review some Smile Later tools. In both cases, and depending on where you live, these tools may have different rules, so make sure to consult with a planned-giving specialist.

Smile Now

These are some tools to help create your tax-efficient legacies now.

Cash

You've discussed the legacy you'd like to create with a charity or foundation, or you decided to finance the legacy project they want to create. You've worked with them to determine a cost, and you wrote a check. Easy. You'll receive a charitable deduction for the amount you give (United States), or a tax credit based on this amount (Canada). In both cases you save income taxes and reduce the cost of your legacy. The legacy is completed. It enhances lives. You smile.

Publicly Traded Securities

So, you bought shares for $1,000 and they're now worth $10,000. Yippee! However, depending on where you live, you'll pay some capital gains tax on that $9,000 gain if you sell them. Instead, you could donate them to the charity or foundation you want to support. In the United States, you'll receive a deduction for their fair market value, provided you have owned them for over a year. In Canada, you'll receive a tax credit based on the fair market value. In both countries you'll pay no tax on the capital gain. The non-profit sells the stock and has the funds to complete the legacy that excites you. You smile.

Shares in a Privately Owned Business

Let's say you own shares in a family business that you began. You may contribute some of those shares and receive a deduction (United States) or a tax credit (Canada). In the United States the deduction is for fair market value, unless you give the shares to a private foundation, in which case the deduction cannot exceed the cost of the shares. In Canada, you'll receive a tax receipt based on fair market value imme-

diately, provided the shares are given to a public charity or public foundation. If they are given to a private foundation, the tax credit is allowed upon the sale of the shares. Whew. All doable, but remember I said, "See a pro."

Tangible Personal Property

This means you donate assets to a charity or foundation that you don't want to maintain or insure anymore, like a car, a boat, collectables, equipment, etc. In the United States, you receive a deduction for the appraised fair market value if the item is related to the purpose of the charity and the charity will retain

it (e.g., a painting to an art museum that adds the item to its collection). If the charity sells the object, the deduction is for the lesser of market value and cost. In either case, you're not taxed on the gain of the property. In Canada, you receive a tax credit based on the appraised fair market value, but you'll be taxed on one-half of the gain unless the object is certified cultural property (see below). The tax credit will always exceed the tax on the gain, resulting in some tax savings. Either way, the charity or foundation knows the legacy you want to create, and it will soon be real. You smile.

Cultural Property

This tool takes advantage of a special type of tangible personal property, recognized in Canada, but not in the United States. Let's say you have a beautiful work of art, a Corinthian statue from 54 BC or a 400-year-old artifact from North America's First Nation's people, something Canada wants to retain as a national treasure. The problem is, there's no room for it in the house. If you donate this object, you'll receive a tax credit based on its fair market value, and there'll be no capital gains tax. Not a bad deal for getting that "junk" out of the garage. You smile.

Donor-Advised Fund

Your request to your planned-giving specialist is simple, "I want to set up a fund where I can make future grants for legacies." This would be a donor-advised fund (United States) or a charitable gift fund (Canada). You can transfer to the charity or foundation that maintains the fund, any asset it agrees to accept, like cash, securities and real estate. You'll receive a deduction (United States) or a tax credit (Canada). Here's the great part: you can recommend grants from your fund to the charities or foundations you want to build legacies with. This tool enables you to make a larger gift when it makes sense from a tax standpoint, and then decide on the big legacy later. As Marvi Ricker of the BMO Financial Group told me, "This is a gift that keeps on giving, long after you're gone." And this is a great way to get your kids involved in your legacy decision-making. You'll all smile!

Smile Later

These are a few money tools to create legacies after you "go"; tools to make it happen later, with tax efficiencies! Sadly, you won't be able to experience them, but you can enjoy your last smile knowing they'll happen. One large estate or planned gift can be transformational for the charitable organization whose values and goals you agree with. They just might be able to create all the legacies you've dreamed of. This is planned giving at its best. You work with charities and foundations when you're healthy, and agree on the legacies you'd like created when some of your resources arrive on their doorstep. You should consult with your financial advisor, estate attorney or planned-giving specialist. As you sing in Saint Pete's heavenly choir, you can smile again as your legacies come true.

Life Insurance

This is a bit of both smile now and smile later. If you have a life insurance policy that you no longer need for family or business purposes, you could transfer ownership to the charity or foundation you've talked legacy with. In the United States, you'll receive a charitable deduction for the value of the policy and for those monthly or annual premiums you'll continue to pay. In Canada, you'll receive a tax credit based on the value of the policy, and for those subsequent premiums. Or you could retain ownership of the policy (just in case you need the cash value of the policy if there's a change in

your circumstances) and name your charity or foundation as beneficiary. If the charity or foundation eventually receives the death proceeds, your estate could realize tax savings. Either way, you'll have discussed with the charity or foundation the legacies you'd like created many years from now when they receive the money. You won't see and enjoy those legacies, but you can smile knowing they'll be created.

Your Will

You leave a bequest (general, residuary, contingency, etc.) to one or several charities or foundations who are clear on the legacies you'd like created after you "go." The bequest could be a specific cash amount, an asset like art or securities, or a percentage of the residue of the estate. In the United States, the bequest will reduce the amount of federal and state estate taxes, if your estate is large enough to be subject to those taxes. If you like this idea and are happy with the other provisions of your will, you could simply add a codicil (amendment) to it detailing this new charitable bequest. In Canada, the charity or foundation will issue a donation receipt for the value of the bequest, which can be claimed to reduce your estate's tax liability. And from yet another place, you smile.

Registered Funds

In the United States, you may have an IRA, 401(k), or a 403(b) plan. If you live in Canada, it's an RRSP or RRIF. If individuals are named as beneficiaries of these funds, sadly those distributions are subject to income tax. In the United States, they could also be subject to estate tax, and the two taxes together could total some 60% of the account value. In both countries, and for legacy-building, you can name a charity or foundation as beneficiary of all or some of these funds. In the United States, retirement funds given to a charity or foundation won't be taxed.

In Canada, the funds will be taxed, however the tax credit will offset the tax, so you can effectively give them to a charity tax free. So, though the rules are different in the two countries, the results are similar: retirement funds make wonderful end-of-life, legacy-building, smile-inducing gifts!

Gift of Residual Interest

This is a cool one, and also a bit of smile now and smile later. Here's how it works. You transfer title to real estate you own to a charity or foundation, but retain the right to use the property for the rest of your life. Without changing your lifestyle, you've just reduced your income tax. Good huh? In the United States, you'll receive a charitable deduction based on the present value of the property the charity will eventually receive when you "leave." This could be your principal residence or a vacation property. In Canada, you'll receive a tax credit for that value, but only if the property is your principal residence.

There are ways to make this work if you have to move for health reasons. Mostly though, you continue to use the property until you and your spouse say "goodbye." Then the charity or foundation sells the property and begins to build your agreed-upon legacies. Yes, you smile!

Gift Annuities

Lots of options here. Did I mention you should talk to a specialist? If your charity or foundation issues gift annuities, you transfer cash or securities in exchange for fixed payments for life, of which a substantial portion will likely be tax free. In the United States you'll receive a deduction for a portion of the assets you transfer, and in Canada you'll receive a tax credit based on that portion. When you finally "go, " the charity or foundation will use your capital to build the legacies you agreed on. One more thing: don't forget to ask about insurance and annuities. Some of the annuity payments to you could be used to buy a life insurance policy. The charity or foundation could be the beneficiary of that policy, or it could be your family, who also know the legacies you'd like created!

Charitable Remainder Trusts

These are more common in the United States, but are possible in Canada. They work like this: You transfer assets – cash, securities or real estate – to a trust. You'll receive a donation receipt for the present value of the remainder that will eventually arrive on the doorstep of your charity or foundation. The amount of the receipt you get will be figured out by those actuaries (math guys), depending on your age, the term, etc.

'You' and 'Legacies'   Trust

In the United States you won't be taxed on appreciated property put in the trust, but in Canada you will be. Well, half of the gain. The tax credit will exceed the tax on the gain, resulting in net tax savings. The trust pays income to you for life (a check every month!), or for a term of years. It will pay either a percentage of the fund or the fund's annual net income. When the trust terminates (and let's say you accompany it), the remaining principal goes to the charity or foundation who knows the legacies you want created. It's a great way to save taxes, perhaps increase your income and make a difference in the future. That's a reason to smile, yes?

Value ➡ Talent/Skill ➡ Resources ➡ Legacy

Okay, I hope I didn't confuse or bore you, but this is good stuff to know a little bit about. These are just a few of many financial tools to help you take advantage of your resources (cash, real estate, stocks, art, etc.) to build your legacies. The structure of these tools can change, as well as their tax implications. But I believe you should first begin with a value that resonates. Decide if you need to use one of your skills or talents, then isolate a resource that will help you build that legacy. Here's the one important question to ask your financial advisor, planned-giving specialist and/or accountant:

"I have this asset and would like to tax-efficiently transfer its value to this charity/foundation, either now or when I 'go.' How can I do that?"

"Real generosity toward the future lies in giving in the present."

– Albert Camus, French author

So, we've been talking about legacy as a very personal endeavor. It gets that way when you're working with your values, skills and talents. All the stories here have generally been about legacy creation on your personal time, but what about at work? I mean, we spend at least a third of our lives at our workplace, whether in the office, the store, the factory or the forest. Can we leave a legacy where we work, and can it be different from what we've been talking about? Hmm…?

LEGACY 9 TO 5
Am I the person my dog thinks I am?

*"It's easy to make a buck.
It's a lot tougher to make a difference."*

– Tom Brokaw

Ever wonder what your dog thinks of you? This is from my colleague, Devon Herndon in Albuquerque, New Mexico:

Every day when I come home, Gus and Yogi, my Australian shepherd and corgi, welcome me as if I'm the greatest human being they've ever met. Sometimes I have to wonder what it is they see in me. But when I look at myself from their perspective, I see the person I want to be.

I'm capable and in control.

I have thumbs and can drive a car and put out fires that start in the toaster oven. I could attempt to build a time machine out of tinfoil and a couple of paper clips, and my dogs would look up in adoration and absolute certainty that I will successfully build it.

I'm patient.

Boy, I'm really pulling a fast one on them with this one. When my dogs look for that perfect spot to relieve themselves, it can take quite a long time until they find it. But I never rush them. Why can't I show the same kind of patience to myself?

I love trying new things.

Once, when walking the dogs, we took an unknown path that cut through a park we had never been through before, but eventually found our way home. I'm sure to them I'm open to unlimited possibilities. I wish I had the same sense of adventure and risk taking my dogs think I have.

I'm generous.

It's while I'm enjoying the most delicious bowl of macaroni and cheese when I notice two sets of pleading eyes on me, and I share my last two bites with Gus and Yogi. To them, I must seem like the most generous human in the world.

I am grateful to have such wonderful companions in my life; ones that make me smile each day, and show me that I have tremendous potential. But I don't always feel like the alpha dog. Perhaps what's missing is the same belief in me that my dogs have. If I just accept their belief, I'd be capable of doing anything I set my mind to.

And now, from dogs to people. *Am I the person I want the people at work to think I am?*

We spend at least a third of our lives working. Whether you're on the shop floor or in a retail aisle, in a delivery truck or a space shuttle, in the basement mailroom or the CEO's 65th floor office, the question is: "Can you leave your mark, your legacy, at work?"

"A person's legacy at work is revealed by how their colleagues and employees think and behave as a result of the time they spent working with you," said Robert Galford, co-author of *Your Leadership Legacy.*

"You're going to leave a legacy whether you like it or not, so wouldn't it be helpful to somehow shape it and articulate it?" says Galford. "My central idea is that your legacy should be a catalyst for how you act today."

A catalyst? You know the values, skills and talents you have to build legacies, what about using them to consciously create a legacy at your workplace? If you're thinking this way, you're living "an examined life that is worth living," and with that comes a sense of purpose. Galford suggests some roles you could play at work:

- Ambassador – a person who handles situations with grace.
- Advocate – a person who is articulate, caring, logical and persuasive.
- People Mover – a team builder, mentor and natural leader who sees people's potential.
- Truth Seeker – a person who has good judgment, is objective, with unquestioned competence.
- Creative Builder – a visionary, entrepreneur and opportunity spotter.
- Guide – a listener and natural therapist helping people to think through problems .

And, there's no problem in asking your colleagues what role they think you could naturally play. The "market" will quickly tell you if you're out of place.

Lucy never got any business.
No one believed her.

"We tend to view legacies as concrete achievements (aka: *stuff*) as opposed to relationships built," says James Kouzes, co-author of *The Leadership Challenge: How to Make Extraordinary Things Happen in Organizations.*

"I think the legacy you leave is the L.I.F.E. you lead," says Kouzes.

Lessons people will say you taught them.
Ideals people will say you stood for, and that they adopted.
Feelings people will say they had when they were around you.
Expressions of your leadership.

These are your accomplishments that benefit all who work with you, and those who follow.

Oh, and values. Kouzes notes that a legacy at work doesn't just appear when we retire. To build a legacy at work, we must be disciplined and intentional about communicating our values, every day. Our colleagues will know what we stand for and will remember what we taught them.

Kouzes' studies also found that we're more committed to our work when we're clear on our values, even if we're unclear on the organization's values. When our values and the organization's values align, we'll be most committed and happy in our work.

Legacy and Leadership

Think of the legacies of Martin Luther King, Ghandi, Nelson Mandela. Yes, they were leaders, and one of their legacies is that they have millions who were moved to continue their work. When you leave your work stronger than it was when you got there, with people who can perpetuate that strength because of your effect on them, the result is a legacy of leadership.

At a dinner for a charity I support, I sat beside Anne and Walter. Walter, 79 and retired, had begun a successful manufacturing company 42 years earlier. Today, daughter Anne was running it.

I asked her, "How does he keep busy?" and she told me.

"Walter, always with a smile on his face, goes in two days a week to our company of 430 employees and spends the day hanging around one work unit – design, fabrication, accounting or marketing. At the end of the day, Walter always finds someone to compliment on their work, and share some stories and history with. He then asks them, 'Where do you want to go? What do you want to learn?' "People love him," she said. "He makes my job easy."

Because I was writing this book, I asked her, "What will his legacy be?"

"He supported people and fostered their growth," she answered, teary-eyed. "And in doing that, he taught others to do it."

We hugged. Walter was looking at us, smiling.

Your legacy as a leader at work will be defined by how others approach work and life as a result of rubbing shoulders with you. When your values and their effect are on display, others will say, "I want to be like that too."

"To me, the most important element of a legacy is, have you helped others build their legacies?" Galford told me. "I advise people to think about this as early as possible in their careers, particularly when they take on leadership roles."

Melanie was a 28-year-old administration assistant working in a big company. She's also a director of the local girls' soccer league. Twelve teams play every Saturday morning. They always need new equipment, uniforms, etc. Melanie, who's not a bad cook either, had an idea. She asked the 12 people in her department to bring some nicely wrapped, homemade desserts the next Friday. At the end of the day, Melanie acted as auctioneer, and the staff bought each other's desserts. They raised $101. There was much laughter and banter. Melanie delivered the money to the soccer league.

A month later, the whole office floor of 52 people had the same auction. They raised $752, and it was delivered to the soccer league too. Spin forward three months and all six floors of the company had an auction. Three years later, $21,450 had been raised and given to local charities. The auctions continue. Melanie says her work legacy is "Teaching people that doing good can be easy, and fun." She's now a senior manager in human resources. Everyone knows she can be counted on to listen to their personal or work ideas, no matter how crazy.

So, go ahead and ask your boss, "What do you want your legacy to be at work?" He or she might not have an answer, but I bet you'll get them thinking.

Then think on this: *What do I want my legacy to be at work? Can I be the person I want people at work to think I am?*

When you're clear on the legacies you want to create at work, look into your dog's eyes and say, "Thanks Buddy. Couldn't have done it without you."

In the early days of settling North America, hunters and woodsmen would often run across the brown bear, the largest land-based predator on earth. Because of this, they would bring their most powerful rifles. They would be *loaded for bear*.

And now you're loaded for bear in legacy terms. You're ready to begin the hunt. If you haven't started already, the next three short chapters will provide the tools and information you need to get started.

GETTING STARTED

Your Legacy Journal

"Everyone wants to live on top of the mountain, but all the happiness and growth occurs while you're climbing it."

– Andy Rooney

The next three short chapters will send you on your legacy-building way. I'll answer some common questions and outline the first steps to take. But most importantly, let's get your Legacy Journal ready to document your journey.

My wife and I each have a small writing pad on our bedside tables. We call them our success journals. The concept is pretty simple: each night before turning off the lights we each write down the date and our successes of the day. For example:

- Had a good meeting with _____ to move the project along.
- Complimented teller at the bank – she beamed!
- Cleaned out the garage tool drawer – finally!
- Got a great rate for a convertible for our trip to the south.
- Great talk with Kath. All is good for our visit next month.

We do this because it's a record of each day in our lives. It's quickly done. It's taught us that every day has successes, even those bad days. And finally, we've found it's good to be addicted to success, no matter what the size.

The Legacy Journal is similar, yet different. It can be a small or large pad, with a fancy leather binding or cardboard cover, your choice. You won't write in it every day, but I believe you'll have a ball reading it as the months and years move on. This Legacy Journal will be a record of what was important to you in your life, what made you happy and what connected you to people. It will contain the stories of your legacies.

I suggest that it has three parts:

1. My Tools
2. My Legacies
3. Legacies I've Seen

1. My Tools

This contains three lists
you assembled:

- Your 10 values.
  ("Raw Materials" page 65)
- The skills and talents you'd like to use or sharpen.
  ("Raw Materials" page 65)
- The resources you could use, when and if they're needed.
  ("Giving Tools" page 185)

This is just a quick inventory of the tools you've already identified that will help build your legacies. This section will change when you add another value or skill that's important to you. The key? This section is the definitive you! It's your inventory of legacy-building tools, and it's good to know what's in the toolbox.

2. My Legacies

This is a description of the legacies you've created, from tiny to humongous. To get started, you could write a short description of the process of TELLING your story – creating your own Legacy Letter. And then your tale of GATHERING – collecting a story that will delight and inform your future family. And then, of course, CREATING your own, unique, separate and powerful legacies. In this journal, write the story of each legacy, including:

- The value you're saluting;
- The skills and talents you took advantage of;
- The resources or tax-efficient tool you used, and what it allowed you to accomplish;
- The people this legacy connected you with;
- The charity or foundation you may have worked with; and
- The real value of this legacy to you, your family, your community and the world. How will this legacy continue to enhance people's lives when you're "gone"?

Over the years, you'll be delighted, proud and entertained as you read through the legacies in your journal. Many years from now when someone is asked to give my eulogy, all they'll have to say is, "This is Robb's Legacy Journal. These are Robb's legacies," and then read them. Simple, neat and powerful.

3. Legacies I've Seen

Jot down those that catch your imagination. You'll find them in the media every day or just by watching others lead their lives. Did this legacy connect people and make their lives better, and will it continue to do that when the legacy builder is gone? Don't be afraid to ask your friends and family about their legacies. Now, you don't want to freak them out with the old, heavy version of legacy (you have to be dead, rich or famous), so have a little fun by using my standard Plains-of-Africa question:

"If you were trampled by a herd of water buffalo, what do you want your legacies to be?"

They may think they don't have any legacies yet, but by asking this question, it focuses them on the future. They have a chance to dream and say, "I'd like it to be this." If they say, "I don't know how to get started," just hand them this book. *One of your legacies will be starting their legacies, and they'll remember you for that!*

We now have our Legacy Journal ready. With it in hand, let's describe our first legacy-building steps.

The First 10 Steps

I can see the lady's face in one of my seminars.

"Tell me what I can do. How can I build a legacy? Just tell me how to start." That request was the reason for writing this book.

You've learned a lot, seen what others have done, and still I understand if you are confused about a good place to start. Perhaps something doable, easy and *you*. Frankly, I'd want exactly the same direction. So, here are 10 realistic, easy, already learned techniques to begin your legacy-building. Follow these 10 steps and you'll begin a process that will ensure a Legacy Smile is often on your face!

1. Ready Your Journal

Have your completed Legacy Journal in hand. Be ready to collect your legacy stories, and other's.

2. Got the Time?

Remember the Legacy Clock exercise we did earlier? I found out I only have 22.5% of my life left, if things go well. Those water buffalo, a speeding bus or a falling chunk of a satellite could get me tomorrow. If you haven't done this exercise, do it now under "Time" (page 36/37). The only moment you've got is now. The next moment is not guaranteed.

3. Values Clear?

Know the values you live by? Sadly, most people don't. You've reviewed your values in your Legacy Journal, and in "Raw Materials" (page 65). Have a look at your values again and pick three that sing to you. You'll start to use them right away.

4. TELL - Legacy #1

Begin your Legacy Letter (LL) by picking one of those values (just one!), then consider:

Why is this value important to me?
How have I tried to live this value?

Congratulations! Your powerful LL has begun. Put your LL away and come back to it when you're ready to write about the next two values. When you've done that, go back to "TELL Your Story" (page 85), and answer some of the other questions; My beliefs? My hopes? What I love? etc. Soon, your LL will be done. You will smile. I promise.

5. The Storyteller?

Who is the one person whose story you don't want to disappear? Talk to your family and decide, then tell that person you'd love to hear their story. Give them the list of areas you want to talk about (e.g., early life, family, school, career, etc.). Confirm with them that it's very important for you, their family, and their family of the future, to know their story. It's all in "GATHER Their Stories" (page 101).

6. GATHER - Legacy #2

Select the person who will talk to the storyteller: you, another family member or a professional. As I mentioned, I think this person will be curious, and be a connector. Decide what media you'll use (audio or video recording). Then begin. Start with a small focus and use that magical, inviting and *I'm interested* question, "Tell me about..." After your first short interview, you'll know there is power as you gather their stories.

7. Talents and Skills

Review your list of skills and talents in your Legacy Journal, or the notes you made in "Raw Materials" (page 65). These are the tools you'll use to create new legacies. Which talents or skills would you really like to use? What new tools would you like to develop as you create a new legacy?

8. Resources to Use

Review the resources you've noted in your Legacy Journal. These are the resources you may need to use if you want to develop a legacy that needs a little oomph – resources like cash, artwork, real estate, etc. Is there one financial tool in "The Giving Tools" (page 185) that looks like a smart one for you? I suggest you talk to three financial planners, then select one who gives you clear answers. And don't forget to select a planner who is also interested in your story.

9. CREATE - Legacy #3

After reviewing your values, skills, talents and resources, what's a small legacy you could create for your family, neighborhood, community or country? Yes, one will come to mind, just like the flowers at the end of the street came to me. Find a person who has read this book to help out, because they get it! Go to sleep telling your brain, *I'd like some legacy ideas!* And, remember why you're doing this. You'll be more connected to others. You'll be happier. Your life will have more meaning. And, most importantly, you'll get to enjoy your legacies *now*, while you're alive. Sounds like a pretty good deal to me. When you've completed your first legacy, no matter what it is, send your legacy story to stories@createmylegacy.com. I'll be collecting stories from around the world, and I'd love to have yours among them.

10. Legacy in the Workplace

Who do all those people at work think you are? What role do you want to play to affect those at work now, which will continue to affect the workplace when you're gone? They're looking at you with those big, brown, cocker spaniel-like eyes. Your values, skills and talents are all on display, there for you to use in a variety of roles. Your workplace is a rich and fertile ground for legacy-building.

I have a feeling you have a couple of questions. Questions you need answered before you charge enthusiastically into your next legacy.

Let me try to answer them.

Legacy FAQs

I'm a little scared to start my Legacy Letter. What should I do?

This is natural. Most of us have self-doubt and wonder if our story has any value. Well, it does. When I started mine, I really wondered where it would go. But, I am so happy now that it's completed. I have a big smile on my face when I open it every six months or so to see if I need to change anything, add a story, etc. *You will only know this if you begin.* Review "TELL Your Story" (page 85). Review those values again. Pick 10 that you believe are yours. You don't have to get them all right the first time; you can change them. Now, pick one value of the 10. Write down why it's important to you and how you've lived it. Put your letter away and I bet that before too long you'll want to get it out and do value #2, value #3, and answer some of the other questions we detailed in chapter 3.

Could my Legacy Letter become my full story, like I'd do for someone else if I was gathering their story?

Yes! It's your story, written by you. You can begin describing some of your values and answer a few questions as detailed in "TELL Your Story" (page 85). Then you can branch out with some of the topics I detailed in "GATHER Their Stories" (page 101). Now you're legacy-building!

I want to gather a story from someone, but I'm too close to them. I really don't think it will work. What now?

First of all, confirm with the storyteller the benefit their story will have for the family now, and well into the future, those who will know who Great, Great, Great-Grandpa was. Ask your family and friends if someone would like to gather that story. If someone is enthusiastic, ask them to read this book. Or, search for a professional and carefully hire someone (see Search Terms on page 234). Take a look at www.createmylegacy.com as we can help you gather and produce that story.

I don't know which values, skills and talents I'd use to create a legacy. How do I decide?

First get them down on paper ("Raw Materials," page 65). Make a list of five values, five skills and five talents. Then, here's what I suggest: look at those lists each day. Remind yourself of what you've got to give. Each morning say to the cosmos, *Hey, I'm lookin'!* Put it out there. It's amazing what will appear before your eyes, or in your thoughts. Also, I remind myself before going to sleep. I look at my values, skills and talents and tell the cosmos, *I'm lookin'!* and then sleep on it. Pay attention to those dreams. They're *you* talking to *you*. Sometimes they point out the obvious, other times a new and intriguing direction.

I know the value, skills and talents I'd like to use to create a legacy, but I can't think of a legacy! Can you help?

Yes we can. Robb Lucy loves meeting new legacy builders. Besides his production company's work in gathering and producing stories, he also consults with those who are stuck, like you. You can have Robb and his team's experience for a one-hour consultation at a small cost. Let us know you'd like Robb to call you to discuss this by emailing stories@createmylegacy.com.

I don't think I could do something like your flowers at the corner legacy because I'm kind of shy.

First of all, do you believe in the legacy you'd like to create? If so, you're more than halfway there. Secondly, most people will respond very positively to your reaching out. Ensure there's a clear vision in your head. Describe that vision to one friend. If they're enthusiastic, ask them if they'd like to help. If they're not enthusiastic, it doesn't mean it's not a great idea, it just means they don't feel the same way. Tell another person. You believe in it, you've thought it through and you'd like to see it completed. Soon there'll be a bunch of people saying, "Yes, let's get it done!" That new community wasn't given to you; you created it. Sometimes we feel like we don't have any power, but you'll be amazed at how many people will join you, and who will thank you and make your vision grow.

Do I have to build my legacies alone?

Nope! You may work alone in "TELL Your Story," but even then you could have someone you love and trust read your story to see if it makes sense to them. I guarantee you'll be closer to that person as a result. You can also join a community or create a community when you're building a legacy. There are many service organizations and clubs who, in their own way, believe in our definition of legacy. I highly recommend you visit your local Rotary International organization, or do an Internet search for "service clubs (your city)."

A mini proverb: *If I have a brick and store it away, it does no good. But if I take that brick and put it into the hands a builder, that builder can add my brick to many other bricks. Soon we will have built something that will bless others long after I'm gone.*

Remember that using your signature strengths leads to increased happiness and connections with people. That burst of happy dopamine in your brain will confirm it's all good, and you'll wear a Legacy Smile.

Does Size Matter?

Your legacy can be of any size if it fits our definition:

A legacy is something I create that connects and enhances lives now, and will continue to positively affect others when I'm gone.

You decide. There's no test, no right or wrong. You can affect people and be happier with a legacy of any size. The following list outlines a myriad of possibilities, big and small.

- A half-page Legacy Letter.
- A new garden in your neighborhood.
- A book on Grandma's life.
- Your resources create 10, 20, 30 years of scholarships for deserving students.
- Your life insurance policy lets a foundation build the legacies you've discussed.
- A school built in a faraway land.
- An addition to the seniors residence.
- Ending the violence in a war-torn country.

If you have any other questions, please send them to stories@createmylegacy.com. I have no doubt the discussion you raise will be helpful for other legacy builders too!

YOUR LEGACY
SMILE 2.0

In a nutshell, I believe that creating and enjoying your legacies with others can bring joy, connection, meaning and fulfillment.

When I visit Ireland, I feel very much at home. If there's such a thing as reincarnation, I believe I lived as an Irishman once. In the late 1800's, my great-grandparents emigrated from South Cork to North America. Oh my, what I'd give to have a Legacy Letter from each of them. Alas, they didn't have this book.

But, they probably bumped into a fellow named George Bernard Shaw, an Irish writer, playwright and co-founder of the London School of Economics. He said what I couldn't say better:

"This is the true joy in life, being used for a purpose recognized by yourself as a mighty one. Being a force of nature instead of a feverish, selfish little clod of ailments and grievances, complaining that the world will not devote itself to making you happy. I am of the opinion that my life belongs to the whole community and as long as I live, it is my privilege to do for it what I can. I want to be thoroughly used up when I die, for the harder I work, the more I live.

> *I rejoice in life for its own sake. Life is no brief candle to me. It is a sort of splendid torch, which I have got hold of for the moment, and I want to make it burn as brightly as possible before handing it on to future generations."*
>
> – George Bernard Shaw

I think this torch is built with our legacies. We can create them with an intentional, positive pursuit, or follow a wandering path leading to who knows where. Being aware of your legacies says you're alive and joyful for what you've done and still want to do. You're asking yourself the questions, *Am I living? Am I loving? Will I leave a mark? Will I matter? Will I be remembered?*

Hmm, sounds heavy. However, it needn't be. As Eckhart Tolle said, "Life isn't as serious as the mind makes it out to be."

So the story of your Legacy Smile is, of course, made up of its W5+H:

The WHO is You

Your story, the stories you collect and the legacies you create, can easily change one life or a thousand lives. Your legacies, large or small, can be transformational. Each legacy will put a smile on your face and be the catalyst for another human being to understand the power of their legacies and the happiness they bring now, and later.

A few months before my old pal Dick left us, I asked him what he thought his legacy was. He looked at me with a long, relaxed smile, and asked:

"What do you think it is?"

I answered, "Thousands who have learned to love the land, take care of it, sharpen a knife, start a one-match fire, build a shelter, dress for any weather, eat heartily in the bush, see the smallest and most fascinating details of nature, to laugh, love, and pass it on, and on, and on."

His smile was bigger. "If that's it, I'm pleased."

The WHAT is Focus

I hope this book has raised legacy-building from your subconscious to your conscious. To not worry about *leaving* a legacy, but to *live* a legacy-focussed life. That's a life with a purpose. When we discover the joy that comes from making a difference in other's lives, we ultimately learn that we are making a significant difference in our own.

The WHERE is Here. Or There

Your legacies can start at home. Your one-page Legacy Letter. A one-hour conversation with Grandma about those old pictures. What does your community need to be enriched? Do you want to affect the big issues on the planet; the health of our land, air and water? The development of our children? Your values, skills, talents and resources will lead you there.

The WHEN is Now

You remember the water buffalo? None of us are guaranteed a tomorrow. As my old friend Hippocrates said, *"Ars longa, vita brevis est."* Art is long, life is short.

The WHY is Your Legacy Smile

You remember my Kilimanjaro climbing buddy, Don? I will remember for a long while the big smile on his face when he told me, "My first value is honesty." He had begun to tell his story.

My Legacy Letter and list of legacies are in my desk drawer. I hope I've got 30 more years of smiles as I create more legacies. As folk artist Grandma Moses said, "Life is what we make it, always has been, always will be."

The HOW is The 10 Steps

We just reviewed them. What step are you on?

Remember that earlier in this book we described a legacy bridge. As we near the conclusion, let's learn of another:

The Bridge Builder

An old man, going a lone highway,
Came, at the evening, cold and gray,
To a chasm, vast, and deep, and wide,
Through which was flowing a sullen tide.

The old man crossed in the twilight dim;
The sullen stream had no fear for him;
But he turned, when safe on the other side,
And built a bridge to span the tide.

"Old man," said a fellow pilgrim, near,
"You are wasting strength with building here;
Your journey will end with the ending day;
You never again will pass this way;
You've crossed the chasm, deep and wide,
Why build you this bridge at the evening tide?"

The builder's voice was rich and mild,
"Good friend, in the path I have come," he smiled,
"There followeth after me today,
A youth, whose feet must pass this way.

This chasm, that has been naught to me,
To that fair-haired youth may a pitfall be.
He, too, must cross in the twilight dim;
Good friend, I am building this bridge for him."

– Will Allen Dromgoole, American Poet, 1860–1934

"AND YOU KNOW THAT WHEN
THE TRUTH IS TOLD
THAT YOU CAN GET WHAT YOU WANT
OR YOU CAN JUST GET OLD."

BILLY JOEL - VIENNA

RESOURCES AND FREE STUFF

There is much information I didn't include in this book, knowing there's plenty here to give you a new perspective on what your legacies can be, and how to begin creating them. If you'd like some extra help to TELL, GATHER or CREATE your legacies, go to www.createmylegacy.com and download for FREE, *The Legacy Starter* PDF. You'll find some helpful elements:

- A list of 400 values to choose from to TELL your story.
- More questions to ask to help GATHER your stories.
- Ideas to help you CREATE your stories.

Simply download the PDF, print it out and add the elements you like to your Legacy Journal. Then tell us about the new legacies you've created by emailing us at stories@createmylegacy.com

Search Terms

There are names of resource websites in this book. But if you'd like to do some searching, especially for local specialists who will help you create your legacies, use these search terms:

Chapter sections	Search Terms
Tell Your Story	Legacy Letter (my city) Ethical will (my city) Personal historian (+ my city or state)
Gather Their Stories	Personal historian (+ my city or state) Legacy production (+ my city or state) Legacy writing (+ my city or state) Legacy stories (+ my city or state) Digital audio recorder Speech recognition software Audio editing software Audio transcription service (+ my city or state) CD and DVD replication (+ my city or state) Photo books, online publishing
Legacy and Money	Planned-giving specialist (+ my city or state) Planned-giving and stories
Your New Dance Partners!	Community foundation (+ my city or state) Charities (+ my city or state) +/- area of interest, e.g., *at risk children,* Arizona
The Giving Tools	Planned-giving specialist (+ my city or state) Planned-giving tools (+ my city or state) Leave a legacy

Acknowledgments

I began talking to people in 2008, with only a vague idea of what a book about legacy would look and feel like. My goal was to simplify the idea and the act of creating legacies. The book changed many times, swinging from a boring scholastic tome to a series of unconnected stories. Most of all though, everyone I talked to helped move it along, give it shape, and confirmed this must be an easy, fun and very useful read. To all my friends and work colleagues who suffered under my repetitive questions, trying to figure out what should be in and what should be out, I owe a debt of gratitude, as I do to the folks who came to my public forums so I could test the content and prod you with that invasive question, "How will you be remembered?"

My warmest thanks to these people who said, "Yes, do it," or "Keep going, Robb, it's worth it."

To Bill Novelli, former CEO of the American Association of Retired Persons, who confirmed in our first conversation that he really liked the idea. And, to his colleague Boe Workman for his ongoing support.

Wilf Wilkinson of Rotary International for his enthusiasm and for putting me in touch with members of an organization that understands, more than others, the merit of *thinking* legacy.

Ross Mayot of the Canadian Association of Retired Persons for his tough love and support on several fronts.

Frank Minton Consulting, LLC for helping simplify those complicated money tools.

Sonny Wong, who said, "I'll help with the blog. It's gotta look good." It does.

Stu Monteith, a brilliant business guy with a heart of gold, and my chief nag from the early days. "Is it done yet, Robb? Huh? Is it?"

John "Tink" Lefebvre, a friend since those days of walking to elementary school (throwing snowballs at cop cars), and a man who continues to help others live better lives.

Kathy Knowles, my unofficial publisher (and official sister who I adore) who was always there. There's value working with someone who knows how your brain works.

Rick Antonson, for that five-hour plane ride, stained napkin and ongoing support. I then watched his enduring legacies grow in the tourism world. Oh, and look for his books.

Kim Lucy, my wife, whose love, encouragement and support ensured you're reading this.

And, to all of these people who let me ask questions and borrow some of their wisdom (and others whose names slipped through the cracks over the years), thank you!

Anielski, Mark, genuinewealth.net
Baines, Barry, celebrationsoflife.net
Berger, Ken, charitynavigator.org
Brignell, Roberta
Cardie, John, checkerscreateskings.com
Chatterton, Phil
Chinalia, Perri, storycorps.org
Cotter, Patrick, bedrux.com
Cowley, Christine, lifegemsbio.com
Deal, Jennifer, ccl.org
Dunn, Elizabeth, ubc.ca
Farnsworth, Scott, sunbridgelegacy.com
Fox, John, memoryminer.com
Franklin, Jason, boldergiving.org
Fraser, Ian, cgfcf.ca
Freed, Rachel, life-legacies.com
Galford, Robert, centerforleading.com
Gilbert, Dan, danielgilbert.com
Gilbert, Tom, Your-Life-Your-Story.com
Gould David, legacyletterproject.com
Grantham Barbara, vghfoundation.ca
Harrision, Scott, charitywater.org
Helliwell, John, faculty.arts.ubc.ca/jhelliwell
Herndon, Devon, devonherndon.com
Howard, Leslie, planforgifts.com
Irvine, Andrew, faculty.arts.ubc.ca/airvine
Izzo, John, drjohnizzo.com
Kanter, Rosabeth, rosabethkanter.com
Kashdan, Todd, toddkashdan.com
King, David, givinginstitute.org
Kotre, John, johnkotre.com
Kouzes, Jim, kouzes.com
Kwasnicki, Meg, imaginecanada.ca
Lambert, Joe, storycenter.org
Lane, Geoffrey, geoffreyxlane.com
Leider, Richard, inventuregroup.com
Leyland, Karen, barnabasfoundation.com

Lyubomirsky, Sonja, thehowofhappiness.com
MacDonald, Diane, cagp-acpdp.org
McElrone, Anne-Marie, cfc-fcc.ca
McKenna, Paul, scarboromissions.ca
McLellan, Joanne, lghfoundation.com
Moore, Dan, guidestar.org
Moulden, Julia, juliamoulden.com
Norry, Marilyn, mymothersstory.org
Offer, Chris, Rotarian, Delta, BC
Ottenhoff, Bob, disasterphilanthropy.org
Pallotta, Dan, danpallotta.com
Pauling, Linda, Chris Greicius' mother
Peterson, Christopher, University of Michigan
Prevost, Roy, royprevost.com
Ricker, Marvi, bmo.com
Roe, Karaleigh, karaleigh.com
Rosenbluth, Vera, linksandlegacies.com
Schendlinger, Mary, geist.com
Schmidt, Buzz, guidestarinternational.org
Schwandt, Hannes, Princeton.edu
Schwartz, Shalom, Hebrew University of Jerusalem
Seligman, Martin, authentichappiness.com
Shankwitz, Frank, a Make-A-Wish founder
Shaw-Hardy, Sondra, womenandphilanthropy.org
Smith, Bradford, foundationcenter.org
Smith, Della, qworkshops.com
Solie, David, davidsolie.com
Somers, Linda, will-help.com
Spears, Marnie, kciphilanthropy.com
Stairs, John, rbcwealthmanagement.com
Steinsky-Schwartz, Georgina, imaginecanada.ca
Stettner, John, worldwish.org
Taylor, Barbara, 2164.net/store/tool/picture-your-legacy
Twyford, Stefani, legacymultimedia.com
Vasquez, Margarita, nicolawealth.com

About the Author

Robb Lucy, known as The Legacy Coach, has always liked adventure. While studying English, business and journalism in university, he sailed the Pacific, then spent time as a fisherman on the Indian Ocean. He's climbed Mount Kilimanjaro and other mountains, kayaked many miles of the Pacific coast, and followed muskox along the shores of the Beaufort Sea.

A natural communicator, Robb is an author, producer and connector. He was a journalist with the Canadian Broadcasting Corporation before forming his own company, producing mixed media for corporations and governments around the world, as well as educational content for thousands of elementary classrooms in North America, Britain and Australia.

Robb spent 25 years on the local, national and international boards of the Make-A-Wish Foundation, and continues to help develop non-profits in literacy, sports history and cancer awareness.

Robb has always found the question, "How will you be remembered?" an intriguing one. He knows the legacies we create give us connections, happiness and a more purposeful life *now*.

Contact Robb at stories@createmylegacy.com to learn about his

- **keynote speeches**
- **conference presentations**
- **consulting on personal legacy creation**
- **production of personal, family and business legacy stories in all media**

Thank you for leaving your review of "How Will You Be Remembered?" in the books category on www.amazon.com

May your legacies cause many smiles!

CPSIA information can be obtained
at www.ICGtesting.com
Printed in the USA
LVOW10s1143070717
540470LV00027B/1002/P

9 780994 031723